Episodes in Archaeology

BARRE PUBLISHERS

Episodes In Archaeology
Bit Parts in Big Dramas

By John Dimick

BARRE, MASSACHUSETTS 1968

ACKNOWLEDGMENTS

The author wishes to thank the following friends for their valued help:

Alton S. Tobey for his fine cover illustration;

Bernard V. Bothmer for his helpful consultations;

William R. Coe, Rodney S. Young, Helen Trik and Richard B. Woodbury for their part in providing the photographs for this publication.

Standard Book Number 8271-6820-9
Library of Congress Card No. 68-29799
Copyright © 1968 by Barre Publishers
Composed and Printed in the United States of America
All rights reserved

Because of her steadfast companionship in often disagreeable situations and conditions, her genuine enthusiasm for my chosen avocation, her so often needed stability and her modest reluctance to disclosure of the extent of her own participation, to Teena with love- - -

The Author

JOHN DIMICK likes to call himself an archaeological buff, a devotee. He has no degree in archaeology and maintains that he is amply comforted by association with numerous confreres who are similarly unendowed yet respected. He became happily entangled with the science in the thirties when he first visited Herculaneum, then being uncovered by the Italians under Mussolini. He laughs at himself, remembering how he was sure at the time he could do a better job. He enjoys telling how, a year or so after Herculaneum in 1939, he was bent on having his own project. He attempted to handle alone a dig in Salvador and after plotting his site and starting to excavate "fell flat on my face" and frantically called for Dr. A. V. Kidder of Carnegie Institution to come down from Guatemala and rescue him and the project.

After that he restrained the urge until after the Second World War, when he embarked upon the restoration of the ruins of Zaculeu in northwestern Guatemala under the auspices and financing of the United Fruit Company. By this time he had learned a lot and he fortified himself with men who knew more.

After that taste of real archaeology and how it should be done, he was hopelessly captivated by the game. He had found his niche in the science or, as he puts it in this account, he discovered bit parts for himself. In relating some of his experiences from then until the present, he emphasizes the inner and less publicized workings of an archaeological program, its organization, its mechanical facets, its financing and the affiliation of those components with the more glamorous aspects usually associated with digging.

Dimick was educated as an engineer. He worked underground in the coal mines of West Virginia and Kentucky, then followed a parental course by joining the engineering forces of Philips Petroleum Company in Oklahoma.

During World War One he was in the Coast Artillery at Fortress Monroe, "safest job in the armed forces." Then eighteen, he was put to laying out barracks and sewer systems for the encampment and "learned a lot about how not to do things."

World War Two found him with his old friend Bill Donovan who shipped him off to Spain with O.S.S. From accounts he did well while making it an exciting experience.

Dimick has the blessing of "good luck" enabling him to create stimulating situations for himself and those associated with him, also a useful and palatable substance for maintaining fervor when it is needed. He has written numerous monographs on archaeology, but this is his first book.

He lives in Washington, D.C.

Contents

Archaeology Defined	1
Some Methods in Archaeology	7
Zaculeu	14
Memphis	65
The Boat Grave of Cheops	86
Tikal	97
"Place where spirit voices are heard"	98
Water	107
The Tomb in Temple One	113
Gordion	
"A City of the Phrygian Kings"	122
Cycladic Interlude	129
Experience in Etruria	140
Epilogue	147
Illustrations following pages	38, 70 and 102

Archaeology Defined

JUST WHAT is archaeology? The cold and unintoxicating definition is "The study of material remains of past human life and human activities." Since Noah Webster published it in 1828 the basic definition has not been altered, understandable when we remember that the science was studied and practiced thousands of years before Webster. School children in the time of Rameses were studying the age of Cheops 1300 years before. Fundamentally, the definition has no need for alteration, but, eyed by the present-day enthusiast, it is unexpressive and descriptively inadequate. Better to say that the definition is outmoded, like describing modern woman by the fit of her bustle. No, archaeology can no longer be so constrictively defined.

Now an amplifying and warmer meaning should be added. It is an urge, an irresistible desire to find and study those remains. Archaeology and its older brother, anthropology, nowadays so stimulate the tyro, the blandly indoctrinated, that, given the chance, he is off and racing to the nearest or most remote site. Vacations include visits to ruins by multitudes of inoculables. The economy of a country is affected. Hotels, restaurants, souvenir shops thrive nearby. Employment is provided for guides, taxi drivers, mule, even camel drivers. Yes, the definition can well be enlarged to include the newer connotation, modern trimming for the original bromidic one.

To observe or listen to old-school archaeologists, one could deduce that none was ambitious to achieve status. The norm among them is to openly play down their very existence, as if they were born out of wedlock. Beneath that cloak of anonymity, however, thrives a self-adoration, a contentment with one's self, equal to any, superior to most. Be sure, then publish.

Nevertheless, there is a glimmer of hope up or down the road. Youth will prevail, the old dogmas will die with their progenitors, or hopefully before, and this beautiful science will thrive on its own. The new breed, the eager graduate student, will raise his hand to be heard, unhappy over that self-protection which has so restricted good deduction. He will ask what would have happened if electronics, medicine, chemistry, had waited until perfection was achieved before students had dared to try or state their theories.

Archaeology has been called justifiably an inexact science. Those involved in it should, no doubt, he comforted that the word science was used at all. If it is an inexact science, or was at the time of that belittling cliché, it most certainly has exhibited an ability to leap to scientific prominence during the past two decades, and still retain its lure for those thousands who cannot resist its thrills.

What other science dares contemplate the consternation of having its precincts so violated, and with such enthusiasm? It is amusingly ridiculous to imagine visiting groups with chemistry primers excitedly wandering through some laboratory where only smells and colored test tubes beckon. With all its publicity, gained

Archaeology Defined 3

from atomic development, can we visualize a physics lab where countless tourists accumulate for tours through the maze of blackboards and slide rules? If we were so arranged in an operating room that we could actually witness what skilled hands were performing within an abdominal cavity, that experience would, no doubt, rival archaeology in its impact, provided, of course, that along with the visual experience the visitor would be given a running account of proceedings. Somehow I doubt the existence of such an arena for the general public.

What has happened to archaeology to so invigorate it? The frightening graybeards with their incomprehensible jargon have dispersed under steady fire from those writers who keep their texts within the realm of understandable reading and still remain factual.

Alfred Friendly recently reviewed *Masada*, by Yigael Yadin. Along with his open praise for the book, Friendly said, "At their most typical, books about the buried past proceed with Prussian top-loftiness, marching in imperious obfuscation and with implicit contempt for any reader who does not share with the learned author an instant recollection of Sennacherib's dates and what he did to Merodachbaladan. The reader perseveres, if at all, only out of intimidation or true love."

In Lincoln Barnett's book, *The Treasure of Our Tongue*, an essay contains among other gems this choice bit: "The author of Academese is usually a specialist in some rather restricted field that he regards as his private preserve. Cherishing his exclu-

ERRATUM

By contrast, family libraries of today will have one or a number of such volumes as: *Gods, Graves and Scholars*, by C. W. Ceram; *Man, Time and Fossils*, by Ruth Moore; *Treasure in the Dust*, by Frank C. Hibben; *Fair Gods and Stone Faces*, by Constance Irwin; *From an Antique Land*, by Julian Huxley; and many others. We are offered today romance, adventure, even intrigue, by modern authors who are well acquainted with their subjects. Illustrated texts have been added to the wealth of good technical writing. Even entire publications concentrate only on magnificent photographs clearly captioned. The recent increase in popularity of archaeology has also been enhanced by the sheer sport of the science. This will horrify some of the old pros, but the most hard-crusted purist among them cannot deny the glint in his own eye which betrays the hope of adventure which may lie just the scrape of a trowel away. His reward may be only the proving of some ancient construction corner or the continuation of a subfloor. But the spirit of the search, the hope of a "kill" is forever there, no transgression upon his academic past or present skills. It has often been said that a "dig" in operation holds far more fascination for the visitor than the completed job. This is somewhat true of the archaeologist. There is something cemeterial about a site once it is finished. The resourceful, if deliberate, movement of the diggers provides the sightseer his thrill, roused further by expectancy of the rewards that momentarily may come to the digger, "a lucky strike," but more likely the result of his knowledge and patience.

Archaeology is a drama of many scenes, backdrops and acts. Costumes have changed but little, purpose always the same. Terminologies of a hundred years ago would be understood and acceptable in today's script.

But the audiences, the readers of the program, the critics, eligible and otherwise, are now legion. The science has been literally rescued from slow death by liberal donations from latter-day enthusiasts. Why? Because we have had to learn that to secure financial assistance from individuals we had to talk understandably and write the same way. The story of the drama, the plot if you like, can no longer be a polysyllabic maze of data decipherable, if at all, by just a few. It can no longer be overburdened with boring footnotes which add the final blast of distraction. Nowadays we have readable accounts of the play, exciting ones, without the slightest infringement upon the factual.

I have struggled, tripped, fallen, risen, missed my cue, even stepped into the footlights during the past thirty years of this healthy transition from the deadly monologue into the inspired narration. . . . just a bit player in a number of big dramas.

A significant departure in archaeological planning during the past ten years has to do with personnel. The age-old digging crew seldom included more than the one expert who set up primitive quarters, hired the local laborers, kept his own house, his notes, his drawings (if any), did his own photography, and was fortunate if he had one beardless student who was little more than a "yes" man.

Today, we have directors, engineers, ceramicists, photographers, geophysicists and a plethora of students. In my case, for instance, as director of the University of Pennsylvania Museum's project at Memphis, Egypt, I didn't know upon arrival, Mendes from Menes. What I did know and what was needed, was how to wrangle with the Arabs for materials, the same technique everywhere, how to see that we got what was promised by the Antiquities Department, how to survey the site, how to use diplomacy when required, and all the extraneous matters which a fine Egyptologist like our Rudolph Anthes simply didn't concern himself with too seriously. But when budgets are low and must be made to stretch, it is imperative that we have management. Such a potion is not always a tasty bit for the archaeological purist. But as the job develops, he becomes progressively more contented with his opportunity to concentrate upon his own specialty and to have someone to whom he can turn for the unscientific requirements. When we undertook the restoration of Tikal in Guatemala I, as director, at once called in a real Mayan expert, Edwin M. Shook, who had spent a quarter of a century with the Carnegie Institution in Maya research in Latin America. He was put in charge of everything having to do with the physical development of the project; my job: get the money, furnish the material and machinery, enlarge the staff, etc. . . . a bit part in the big drama, actually a sort of off-stage voice.

On the Greek island of Kythera Aubrey S. Trik and I joined Professor George Huxley, Professor of Greek at Queens University in Belfast. Huxley had had only moderate field experience at that time but he is an archaeologist who is in such complete command of his subject that he makes it all look easy. Later, I will discuss George and Kythera but there he and his little island site represented just another example of the necessity for a diversified force. Trik had been with Carnegie Institution during the restoration of Copan in Honduras and was Chief Archaeologist at our restoration at Zaculeu. I did the survey at Kythera and Aubrey Trik did the grave exploration and recording, both small parts in the broad historical complex which covered some three thousand years of occupancy from Minoan to Hellenistic to Roman. But without our comparatively small contribution, the dig at Kythera would have been just another search for historical material. The modern archaeologist, such as Huxley, welcomes the bit player. There are only a few of us. At our curtain call, if we should ever have one, our bows will be towards the young and confident prinpals.

Some Methods in Archaeology

Ask an expert archaeologist, "How do you dig?"—his answer will be another question, "Where?" Good tactics for the approach and handling of any given site are as varied as those of a surgeon who is asked how he operates. The same man is skilled in appendectomy, vagotomy, kidney ailments and other operative problems distributed over the body. His technique, however, depends upon the area to be explored, studied and restored. Not every handling problem of digging is different at the start but it may well develop its own peculiarities and eccentricities as it unfolds.

The geophysical instruments available to the archaeologist today are comparable to the X-ray and its capabilities for assisting the surgeon. The magnetometer, which will be discussed later, sends its pulsations down into the earth, searching for man-made obstructions which, when encountered, are reflected on the dials of the operator above much as the fluoroscope discloses irregularities in the body and flashes them on the screen for the surgeon. And, as the surgeon, once convinced, makes his incision in the proper place, so does the digger, fully aware that an anomaly (term used in this case to denote any deviation from normal) is there, but unable to diagnose it positively without looking at it and feeling it.

As surgery once had to function without X-ray, depending solely upon symptoms and instances of similarity, so did and does the archaeologist. First and most frequent aids are symptoms, and the best examples of those are manmade mounds. When discovered, they may be grass-covered, overgrown with brush, even trees, or smothered with windblown silt stopped there and piled up by the structure itself, long ago deserted. Cleverly disguised by nature's insidious processes, a mound may have every appearance of being natural. If it stands alone, as mounds often do, lending no clue by a conformation with others, the digger must probe its base and slopes, looking for telltale evidences of past human presence or occupation. Such proofs may be flint chips, broken stone from a neolithic period, shaped bone fragments such as needles, or bits of pottery (potsherds). Often only a handful of any of these symptomatic objects, or even less, is ample evidence.

Mounds in clusters or in obvious alignment of course leave no doubt of their origin. Nature dislikes and avoids straight lines and architectural conformity. Man introduced straight lines and sharp angles. Nowadays mound groups occur in areas whose history is at least partially known and recorded. The knowledgeable digger knows in general what to expect; his hopes and purposes are to improve the record, enlarge it, possibly correct it.

First the mound is cleared. It is then surveyed both for shape and elevation. The resulting map and profile largely determine the method of attack.

If the mound is a low, spreading type, the most accepted plan of exploration is to mark off the surface into large squares, possibly three meters or ten feet. The squares are exactly located on the general plan and firm stakes driven at the corners. As many of these "quads" as there are individual diggers available may

Some Methods in Archaeology

be started, sometimes more. Such a method makes for well controlled excavation. Each object or anomaly as encountered can be located quickly and accurately by intersecting measurements from any two corner stakes. Changes in the overburden or covering earth can be plotted by vertical measurement down from the surface where elevations were taken before the start.

So the large mound begins to resemble a huge checkerboard. The narrow walls separating the quads are lowered as the depth of the working areas increases. Finally they will be removed entirely, leaving the sections combined into one large exposure. The notes and drawings of each quad will be fitted together and the entire exploration can be properly drawn to scale and made ready for study and publication. How many of these quads and how much of the mound's surface is explored is governed by results as they occur, and the intelligent prognosis as to what may lie ahead or further down. The wise archaeologist is hesitant to quit until he is convinced that he has explored all possibilities down to sterile soil. Like the surgeon again, he has made the incision, now is the time to examine all possibilities.

Building walls, however mundane and uninteresting, must be given full respect. Structural evidences must receive the same care as a rich burial and must be recorded with exactitude in order that the draftsman's final rendering will be an accurate small scale of that mound, from its grass roots down to its final floor. The draftsman may be thousands of miles away in an office. All he will ever see is what the digger brings back. Disconnected finds must be sketched, photographed and their locations marked on the field map. Every shred of evidence, from signs of wrecked and deserted floors to soil changes, is detailed on the field notes of the trained archaeologist. Decisions on general chronology as well as occupation sequences often depend upon the accuracy of those recordings. Carbon 14 or other scientific dating methods will later be applied to specimens to help confirm their relevance to other materials found above or below. Thus our mound has undergone its surgery. Unless the structure found within is to be restored, the gaping wound will be closed by refilling, and later explorers who come upon it, be they properly prepared by reading, will know that everything worth knowing about that provocative looking mound has been learned and published.

Our next mound is not a low flat one, but a steep-sided higher one. The quad system is not adaptable. The checkerboard is not playable on a steep slope. The same clearing and base study with elevations must be made. If there is strong evidence that the mound covers the eroded remains of a building, the archaeologist in his examination of the base will search for signs or architectural features, such as an entrance or an outside stairway, which could indicate what had been the front. If there is no such evidence the next best plan is by orientation. Experience and records may show such buildings to have been erected on a north-south or an east-west axis. Let us assume that an east-west axis is decided. The base survey and elevation completed, the digger lays out his trench from the east side and proceeds toward the mound at its base, or at a floor level if one has been found in the front. His recordings and mappings en route are the same as for the flat mound except that he is now working horizontally instead of vertically. His two side walls become higher above him as he probes further into the mound, away from the sloping exterior.

Suddenly the stub walls of his hoped-for structure are revealed. Just as if he had reached an impenetrable barrier, the digger must alter course. Cautiously this archaeological sleuth follows his evidence which may be soft and crumbly and only an inch or so high. He hopes for a corner now or better still, a doorway which will lead him to the interior and will also tell him the wall thicknesses. On and on the methodical process continues, no drama here, no excitement, just plain, tedious, devoted work. Floors are carefully swept in the search for cuts which may lead to burials. Every scrap of material, worthless intrinsically, is examined and marked in an effort to learn the age and relationship of the building. Artifacts found under a floor can be marked older than the floor, those on top contemporary, older or younger. Burials cut into a floor and then sealed are therefore younger than the floor; those buried and the floor placed over are of necessity older; and so the mound unfolds its mysteries.

Field notes of the archaeologist become treasures, irreplaceable if lost or destroyed before they are transcribed. The men of Carnegie Institution first used field books with carbon copies. The copies were removed regularly and forwarded to the main office for fear of the irretrievable loss of the originals. Aubrey Trik's field drawings are artistic gems. We actually have one of his working sketches framed and hanging in my wife's dressing room.

There are innumerable departures from these fundamental basics of mound digging. Nuances occur, brought about by conditions, like tunneling which was done successfully at Tikal in Guatemala and Gordion in Turkey. But the theorem prevails; the system, plus knowledge of the ancients and consequent recognition of what is recovered, are tantamount to success.

Not all digging involves mounds. Many of the world's most exciting archaeological adventures provided no earthworks to guide the searchers. The tombs of the Pharaohs were skillfully hidden and camouflaged into the desert rock and sand. The flat plains of Sybaris in southern Italy still refuse to surrender a trace of where that paragon of luxury once stood. Jericho's remains gave no more clues to its whereabouts than would a kleenex under your blanket. Archaeological history presents a succession of quests for concealed intelligence, some successful, others frustrated. But the methods, the processes of the scholar, retain their pattern. They also make the same intellectual demand, a foreknowledge of the subject and the object of the search.

In the desert sands of Egypt or the powder-fine dust of the

Holy Lands, digging resolves itself into a laborious removal of those windblown elements from where they have accreted themselves against what we hope are manmade baffles below. Dark men in white cotton robes with baskets holding half a peck of earth form a chain which twists and writhes slowly but everlastingly to the dumping ground; then back with empty baskets, but with no change in pace, for another load. The western digger is at first provoked to restless exasperation by the cadence of these men, who have learned over the centuries just how much energy per minute should be expended under the desert sun. By day's end our westerner concedes the obvious growth of the refuse area.

The quarry, if it exists at all under these flat sites, only a dot on the map, may be as much as fifty feet under this heap of nature's materials. But, once committed to a site, the archaeologist is reluctant to desert it. Bedrock will tell him of his failure. His final elevations will then be taken, his search in vain. But when his trowel comes upon evidence of earlier man's house or his arena or his city wall, the same prescribed methods are called for: follow, record, deduce *and* report. No archaeology is worth its name if the results are not made available to others by the printed word.

Another, a sort of Orphan Annie to some in archaeology, is the science of digging house mounds or localities which were home sites. This grubby work holds none of the glitter, the thrill, or hopes for the valuable rewards of rich burials and palaces of the ancient plutocrats. However, it is essential to proper exploration. How did the ordinary citizen live? What tools did he have, how and what dishes did his wife prepare? What animals are represented by the bone fragments strewn on that earthen floor? And dozens of other ponderables.

The mud-walled huts of the poor are usually eroded to inches. A charred hard spot on the floor marks where the home fire burned, its smoke drifting out through the open eaves.

Such digging is painfully realistic and humdrum, but must

be done with the same meticulousness and skill and foreknowledge as in the more glamorous areas. Little may be unearthed, but what is learned throws some light on the vast majority, the ancient peasantry. When you watch a scholar on his knees, with small knife and trowel tenderly scraping away at an earth floor, you are observing a dedicated archaeologist, no drama there except by his own standards. His rewards may be only his satisfaction with a job well done and the resultant recognition by his fellows.

Zaculeu

INTERNAL Revenue looks with disfavor on Country Club dues as a deductible item, but the links and the locker room are often powerful allies in swaying the fickle buyer. Pat Partridge and I were neither buyer nor seller, just two friends about to have a Sunday morning round on the south shore of Long Island.

The time, Spring of 1946. Normalcy was jadedly returning to a tuckered world. But in our country, typically, adjustments were rapidly taking place. On the bench by the first tee, Zaculeu Project had its conception. Pat was an old-timer with United Fruit Company. He was the guiding genius and sparkplug of the recently created Fruit Dispatch, the marketing side of the United Fruit Company. Chiquita Banana was his dream girl.

Pat knew of my keen interest in archaeology.

"John," he said, "it seems to me that the United Fruit Company would be interested in helping develop some ancient ruin in Guatemala where the company has been operating successfully for so many years. After all, they have built hospitals and schools and have gone to great lengths to, shall we say, pour a bit of wine back on the ground from whence they have taken the grape."

"Furthermore," said Pat, "our company is still being lashed by the excess profit tax and any donation for educational purposes such as archaeology would be paid for with what amounts to about a ten cent dollar."

"But Pat," I inquired, "whom would I approach in United Fruit?"

"Only one man," said Pat. "Samuel Zemurray. He has a long-standing love for the Latin American countries, maintains a home in Honduras, and is Chairman of the Board of the company."

"Is Mr. Zemurray a difficult man to see?" I asked. "Yes," purred Pat, "he is. You must telephone his office, say you want to talk with him, and he will probably tell you to come on down right away."

On the following morning on my way into New York, I resolved to call this man. I phoned his office at Pier Three, North River, New York, shortly before ten.

His Boston-bred secretary embarked on the usual formalities: What is your name and what company do you represent and does Mr. Zemurray know you . . . to none of which questions did I have an adequate reply. Desperately I remembered that I did know Mr. Zemurray's daughter, Doris Stone. I threw that into the breach and received the slight encouragement "Hold on please."

In a moment Mr. Zemurray was on the phone.

I heard a deep voice with pronounced accent say, "And what can I do for you?"

At that point, I decided to take the whole plunge.

"Mr. Zemurray," I said, "I want to do an archaeological restoration in Guatemala and I want to come down and talk with you about it. When may I come?"

His reply left me speechless. "Can you be here in half an hour?"

Weakly, I answered, "Yes, Mr. Zemurray," and received his final "All right," followed by a firm disconnect.

I hailed a cab from uptown and fifteen minutes later I was pacing Samuel Zemurray's outer office.

While composing myself by looking at the scenes of banana plantations and photographs of ships which composed the Great White Fleet, I realized how ill prepared I was for this meeting and how. as is my temperament, I had plunged into a promotion which, if given more preparation, might have had some chance of working. One day given to the background work could have meant success, as against this brash approach which must result in almost certain failure. But asking such sanity from me, by me, was too alien to my pattern of behavior and there was nothing to do now but full throttle ahead. The time had come —

The secretary, with a curt, "This way, please," escorted me down a long hall to an open door and into a large room with a huge desk in the far corner, behind which sat the man. I was scared.

During the following four years, as I grew to know and respect this man, all of my first impressions deserted me.

But that morning, I looked across the table at a broad-chested character whose hands, doubled into big fists, were poised to drum the desk, whose features, bronzed and wrinkled, belonged under the tropical sun, not in the office of a Board Chairman. I saw a muscular torso, a large round head and a frightening combination of the two.

How could this be the man who only an hour ago had said "Come on down"?

Here was a living unimpugnable specimen of man who had come up the hard way.

If we were equipped with all the facts, all the exciting anecdotes, all the truisms which went into the early life of Samuel Zemurray, and could follow up with his adult life, his blooming into eminence in Latin America and his final leap to the very top of his chosen field, raising and marketing of bananas, it would be far more bountiful to produce that biography than this story of archaeology.

Someday Doris Stone may find time to write of her father. Not only is she able as a writer, but she alone knows the facts, the personalisms and the human side of that remarkable man. A sketch here may kindle the reader's desire for more:

When I stood in his office that spring day in 1946 realizing that he was absolute monarch of that complex company, United Fruit, I commenced to recall the bits of his early life which had come to me from dependable sources years before.

Samuel Zemurray came to this country in 1892. Little was known of his antecedents except that his father was a poor Bessarabian farmer. He began his life in America under protection of an uncle and aunt who had come over earlier. The uncle ran a tiny country store in Selma, Alabama, and at the age of fifteen Samuel started to work for his uncle. His pay, at most, consisted of his food and lodging plus the opportunity to learn English. (He kept his strong accent during his entire life.) But working for another was, even then, repugnant to Samuel. He was constantly searching for his own devices.

Bananas were beginning to appear in quantity on the wharves of Alabama ports by that time. But refrigeration was poor, if it existed at all on the ships, and a significant percentage of the fruit was too ripe for extended rail shipment when it arrived.

Jobbers were dealing with local merchants for disposal of the overripe fruit for resale near at hand. Any price obtainable was salvage for the jobber.

Zemurray saw his opportunity to get into a business which, although it was not exactly farming, dealt with a farm product.

He was on his way to become the continent's greatest expert on raising bananas.

Ships were throwing overboard in the harbor of Mobile entire stems of fruit which contained, at times, only a small percentage of over-ripe bananas. Samuel would row out and gather those stems, cull them himself. He was also buying from the quick-dealing jobbers. And, in short time, his skill in selection put him in position to ship some of his fruit to nearby cities.

His reputation spread. He knew his business and soon he was making deals with other small companies for merging. It was no wild guess who would run the merged groups.

Ashbel Hubbard, earlier far more influential in the fruit business than Zemurray, came into his flock. Thatcher Brothers Steamship saw the advantages of having this rising agricultural and business genius, Zemurray, on their team but they could only get him by merging and giving him the gavel. This they did.

All of this successful wheeling and dealing was thunderous excitement for a man who had to look back only a few years to a cot in the attic and a six A.M. awakening to sweep out the small store.

But the weariless urge from his background still prevailed. The production game was his. By 1905, he was off to the land whence came his bananas: Honduras.

The Honduranians were not aware at first just what Zemurray's entrance meant to them. That beam in his eye was focusing on the rich lands along the Cuyamel River, or a railway which would carry away his own fruit, and on a strong hand in whatever government considered itself the power at the moment.

As 1910 closed, Miguel Davila was President of Honduras. Even had his country been prosperous, he would have been no match for Zemurray. But broke he had no chance.

Zemurray knew what he wanted: consistently low taxes, permits to build when and where he chose, including a railroad, and duty-free imports on all material and equipment necessary to his plans.

Davila sealed his own doom when he opened negotiations with New York bankers for a loan to save his country.

Right off, the bankers insisted upon complete control of customs and to insure control, to have their appointed customs inspector there as watchdog. Zemurray's free imports plan could be the first to be thrown out should the bankers sign with Davila. It took Samuel Zemurray a moment only to sense that not only he but many local dissidents were against such mortgaging of income.

General Manuel Bonilla, who had sat in the precarious seat of President at an earlier date, headed a faction which had little use for Davila. Bonilla was then in exile in the United States. Soon he and Zemurray were head to head in New Orleans, their purposes identical, their reasons just divergent enough to insure a camaraderie: Get rid of Davila quickly. This sort of conclusion in Latin America implied just one instrument, overthrow.

Bonilla had been overthrown long before Honduras contained sufficient wealth to afford him opportunity to accumulate a private and exported fortune. He had nothing except an existence income in America. Now he had Zemurray.

Zemurray helped him purchase on old yacht called the *Hornet*. Its condition was anything but sound, but it should hold together for a normal passage to Honduras. Honduranian funds came also to Bonilla from Zemurray's purse. Rifles, ammunition and a machine gun were stored aboard at night.

Zemurray owned a small cruiser which was brought into use for shore-to-ship transfer. Certainly the U.S. Secret Service had some knowledge of what was transpiring. There may have been means for causing heads to be turned away, but there is no proof positive.

All went well with the loading and finally Zemurray saw the yacht take off with only Bonilla and two friends, who went along just for the adventure, aboard.

But the next President had planned well. He put in at Puerto Cortes where stout men who loved him were waiting to get aboard.

In no time, Davila was a living has-been and Bonilla was back in power. The loan plans with American bankers were quickly cancelled and Zemurray's wishes were commands to the new President.

During my own years in Guatemala the usual derogatory comment on the Fruit Company was invariably sweetened with stories of how it had conquered the Latin Americas by force. That is not only unjustified, but untrue.

The conquistador was Zemurray. He with his wisdom, his love for the country as well as for self-benefit, was the power who employed the force of arms.

However it is examined, and with whatever personal like or dislike historians may express toward Zemurray, it must stand that what Zemurray wanted for himself and his company was ultimately worthwhile for the political arena in which he fought. It was many years after this last incident that the United Fruit Company purchased Zemurray's interest and became a factor in Latin American business and political life.

Before this vital personality impressed himself upon the agronomy as well as on the economy and politics of Meso America, bananas were taken almost wild. Cultivation and improvement were considered as unnecessary expense. Pick out the good, throw away the bruised. Ship at once and get what the market would offer, like pelt marketing in the old West.

Sam Zemurray was a farmer with a farmer's urge to grow anything bigger, hardier and more abundant. At first this knowledge and energy were difficult for the native to appreciate. But as results multiplied and Zemurray's natural manners and fairness more and more impressed the native growers, his popularity grew and their confidence in him solidified.

He freely put back into the land his profits, often his own

before profits. He ventured into large-scale irrigation to develop lands which had heretofore been considered waste. Fertile silts which had always gone down the rushing streams, wasted into the seas, were flooded over the land to deposit themselves and produce constantly improving stems.

As the stems grew stronger and the banana weight increased, the pithy plants could not hold them. Bamboo was everywhere. Zemurray had his men cut the poles and prop up the sagging plants under the stems, thus preventing them from touching the ground. Thousands of stems each season were saved by this simple expedient.

He lived and worked among his bananas and his chosen people. He was always on the job. He made the decisions and gave the orders.

While uncertain farm managers of United Fruit elsewhere were groping for answers and telegraphing to Boston for decisions, he was guiding his own destiny. Zemurray's Cuyamel Company had arrived. This simple, dedicated farmer from the Near East was the dominant figure in the banana business of Central America.

More and more acres swelled into fertility under his genius. He reached northwest into the Motagua Valley, his concessions from Honduras coming to him now just for the asking.

Motagua land was a questionable territory. It was precariously on the border between Honduras and Guatemala. Had it not been for the ever increasing ambitions of Zemurray for more lands to develop, that section would have been overlooked for years to come.

United Fruit had all the lands it could systematically operate at that time. It sought no further spreading beyond the recognized Guatemalan border. But once Cuyamel challenged, old scars were rubbed raw between the two countries. Border lines which had been only mildly in dispute for half a century became cause for conflict. If the land was Guatemala's, then United Fruit had good claim. If not, it was up for grabs.

Both sides' troops were like something from a Gilbert and Sullivan operetta, mostly barefoot, ill equipped and loath to fight. They snarled at each other across what was a supposed boundary, let go sporadic shots, probably drank together in the evenings.

Affairs such as these have usually been worth only their effect on the urban populations where large numbers could be swayed by the threat of outside enmities, thus distracting them from their internal ones. But here the solution was imminent.

In 1929, before the desperate economic plight of the United States was far enough along to jeopardize such a deal, United Fruit came to terms and bought out Zemurray and Cuyamel for 300,000 shares of United Fruit Company stock. Worth at the time of closing over thirty million dollars, it was not an insignificant dividend for a young Bessarabian for fifteen years' work.

Typical of the man and his devotion to the banana industry, Zemurray gave no thought to diversification of his holdings. Within a few disastrous months his fortune had dwindled because of the collapse of the market, and United Fruit stock was a tenth of its value when acquired.

But frustration was not accepted complacently by this man. Not only was he the largest stockholder of United, but by this time he had a following of other holders. The Harvard-educated and Boston-bred executives of the Company were not accustomed to men like Zemurray, brusque to a degree of insolence, fully in command of his subject and intolerant towards white collars, silver spoons and Minton china.

At the next meeting of the stockholders, those men were in for a rude shock. Zemurray laid his stock and his proxies on the table and pronounced himself in charge of operations. Many a proxy appeared in that exposure which shocked the blue bloods of Boston. But the time had come to change horses, even for those whose financial omnipotence had never before been challenged.

With full control, Zemurray gave up the luxury of his recently acquired home in New Orleans and moved back to Latin America. Old buddies who owned Fruit Company stock, to the exclusion of any other security in some cases, welcomed him.

Plantations were restored to the old and successful method of a free hand for the managers, with energetic restlessness and determination to get the job done. Blights were becoming a menace and had to be dealt with. They were. Whole sections had to be abandoned at least temporarily until those plagues were eliminated.

But the man of the hour had returned and victory gleamed upon his banner. Fruit Company stock jumped 160 per cent on the news that Zemurray was in the field. The step from Managing Director to Chairman of the Board was easy and natural. And this was the man whom I was facing that Monday morning in 1946.

The war had ended, but the surtaxes were still in force. United Fruit, like many other corporations, could spend dollars for tax-exempt projects at a cost to the corporation of only a fraction.

There was no time now to appraise this powerful man, who at once inquired, "Now, young man, what's this about archaeological work in Guatemala?"

"Mr. Zemurray," I replied, "I want to take one or two of the recognized experts in Meso American history and archaeology to Guatemala, make a survey with them of the available sites built by the Maya, have them advise me on what and where we could work. Then with the help of these men or others whom they recommend, do a restoration of the selected site in the name of the United Fruit Company. Such a monument would perpetuate the name of the Fruit Company for centuries to come.

"From available records of similar projects in Latin America under the aegis of foundations I can, by adding an understandable percentage, come up with a fairly accurate estimate of the costs. I would like to project the work over a three year period and give you an annual estimate in advance." I liked the way he paid attention.

"Before we can talk further," Mr. Zemurray said, "we would have to have a prospectus. How long do you think it would take you to give me a fairly detailed account of the costs, and how you plan to conduct the work?"

It was then just mid-morning and I heard myself say, "I'll have it here by two o'clock this afternoon."

Sam Zemurray's glance portrayed a combination of surprise, skepticism and satisfaction. He ended the interview by pushing his chair back from the desk.

I was staggered at the extemporaneousness of it all when he suggested that I leave my name and address with his secretary on the way out. He didn't even know my name. One wild commitment on my part was following another in frightening sequence.

Riding high, I gave no thought to an ebb tide. I jumped into a taxi in front of the pier. "Savoy Plaza, in a hurry, any route."

Up the West Side Highway, over Fifty-eighth Street to Fifth Avenue, and we were there in fifteen minutes.

The public stenographer at the hotel was an old friend, a veteran of my stenographic whims many times before. She was accustomed to my abrupt and unheralded entrances.

When I flopped down beside her desk and explained the emergency, she was not too surprised.

There was no time for rewrites or corrections. This prospectus had to stand on its first edition. Somehow the dictation seemed to catch my enthusiasm and flow along smoothly. I made no attempt to multiply weekly estimates by four, or monthly estimates by twelve, or yearly estimates by three. Not only did I deal in round numbers, but in rounded thousands.

The more I dictated, the more necessitous items heretofore unthought of stood forth and demanded inclusion.

Finally, after a half hour of steady dictation, the stenographer's pages leafed over more slowly and I realized that all was said that was worthwhile and any further embellishment would be redundant. Any detail or cost item forgotten would have to come out of the percentage factor usually allowed in even the best prepared estimates.

Having gone this far on sheer brashness, I decided to go the whole way and added my last item, ten per cent of the above for unforeseen costs.

"When do you want this?" asked my girl Friday, leafing through her shorthand.

"By one-fifteen," I answered.

"But what day?" she asked.

"Today."

"You'll have it," she said, unblinkingly.

"I'm going for some lunch," I told her. "I'll send yours up. What will it be?"

"Bourbon on the rocks, a club sandwich and coffee," came the automatic reply.

Leaving my raincoat and hat in her office, I was off to the dining room. When I opened the menu and looked at the items with the prices extended to the right, the agonizing realization struck me that I had no idea what that document upstairs was going to amount to. How big was *that* check going to be? Would the customer lose all appetite when he regarded my hastily concocted menu?

Suddenly, I was aware that with the exception of this one waiter hovering uncertainly over me, I was the only person in the dining room. No doubt this patient man expected me to order breakfast. It was then not twelve.

Making some sort of mumbled apology, I retreated into the lobby, bought a noon edition of the *Telegram* and battled with my preoccupation until noon and promptly went to the bar.

Two bourbons and a clam stew later, I was back upstairs.

Nonchalantly, as if this were an everyday occurrence, my wonderful friend handed me four beautifully typed legal sized pages, in triplicate, a little necessity I had completely forgotten to order.

"It's been proofread, too," she said. "Any mistakes on those pages are your own. The next time you bring me a job, don't give me so much time. You make me lazy. And please, no long compliments — I've work to do."

I decided to spare myself the shock of the total until I was in the taxi and headed downtown. Crossing Fifty-seventh Street, I still restrained myself but became more disquieted by guessing.

At last when we were squared away and headed down the West Side, I turned to the last page. What lay before that, the details making up the final, mattered very little. I found myself staring at $430,000.00 for the three year venture!

What would Samuel Zemurray say? There was no precedent for such a figure in Western Hemisphere archaeology, only one or two in the world. There were no guidelines, no comparisons to be made. I decided that this was a help.

Nervously, I flipped through the preceding pages, but had already decided that, with a man like Zemurray, they would mean very little. He would either buy my idea and me or he would not. What did it matter if food and transportation, for example, turned out to be far more than my estimate, and labor less. It would all be in the one colossal pot in any case.

Right on time, I re-entered Mr. Zemurray's office.

Without comment, I handed him the original. He thumbed the first pages in a fashion which convinced me that I had been right; he was looking for totals. He came to the last page.

I will never forget that moment and what Mr. Zemurray said.

With a sly wink, he said, "Well, young man, I will have to take this up with my Board of Directors."

He continued, "I think it's a pretty good idea. If we decide to finance the project, when do you want to begin?"

"If I have your answer, sir, by the first of August," I said, "I would like to be on the ground in Guatemala by September first."

"You will have it before that," he said.

Only four hours earlier he had asked for my name and address.

What magic was this? How had the gods on that spring morning so composed themselves to bless this idea? In the short time from ten until two-thirty, the plan had been proposed, detailed and, I believed, had gone fairly well on its way toward being accepted. Nothing to do now but wait.

In mid-July, I received a formal letter from United Fruit stating that the sum of $143,000.00, one year's budget, would be deposited to my credit with the Guatemala City office of the Company, to be mine when the selected site was approved by the Company.

My first move was instinctive and automatic. Call Dr. A. V. Kidder in Cambridge!

Ted Kidder was then Director of Carnegie Institution for Archaeological Research. He controlled, at that time, a handsome budget. His enviable reputation as an expert on Latin American pre-Columbian history was worldwide.

But he had so much more, a tolerance and understanding unique in the profession. I knew that Ted would be pleased that this United Fruit restoration was planned for Guatemala.

His knowledge, coupled with his enthusiasm, were what I needed quickly.

"Ted," I said, "I have found the funds to do a sizable restoration and research in Guatemala. I need your advice on where to work, whom to hire as archaeologist and architect, and all the side advice you will please volunteer."

I filled him in on what I had done with United Fruit and I hoped I could sense his interest mounting.

"When do you plan to go down?" asked Ted.

"Just as soon as you and your people can be ready," I replied.

Good sense then prevailed and he suggested we meet in Guatemala City in mid-August.

He and his wife, Madeleine, met me there and introduced me to Ledyard Smith who was to go along. Ledyard was an old pro with Carnegie. He probably knew the Maya territory as well as any man and had dug with such success that his "luck" was legendary.

I soon realized that this tour was not one to educate me to the scenery of the Guatemalan Highlands enroute to our area of exploration. We passed, without comment from anyone, beauties of nature and man which, had I been on an escorted tour, would have consumed hours of description and investigation.

Antigua, for instance, the early capital of the Spanish colonials, was left with a dusty swish of the car stern. Its more than a hundred fine remains of churches and cathedrals received no mention.

Atitlan came in for a bit more respect only because we spent the night there. The lake with its necklace of volcanos by sunset was an arousing spectacle.

Madeleine, with the nonchalance of a seasoned visitor, told me of the villages on the far side of the lake where one could behold the Indians performing their daily chores in dress and fashion of old. Later I went many times to those villages and never ceased to add something to my knowledge of them.

Next day we were off to the land of the Quiche Indians via Chichicastenango where every tourist for a half-century has visited and experienced the first real taste of the life of the Highland Maya.

With, from Madeleine, a cursory "The only important days here are market days, Thursday and Sunday," she let me know that this again was only a temporary stop. We dined early, were in bed by candlelight and off the next morning. Indians were still asleep on the sidewalks as we departed.

The upland country from Chichicastenango northward is dotted with small clusters of grass-covered mounds, probably individual burials. These we passed without comment and by noon had come to our first view of the deep valley of the Rio Negro. This prankish, twisting and unpredictable stream one minute would be vigorously cutting away at the side walls of its bed, and the next would slowly caress a flat sand or gravel bar with pond-like serenity.

The car stopped after a moment and I was invited to alight and have my first view of one of the ruins we were to contemplate.

On the far side of the stream, the bank rose in a sheer bluff some two hundred feet high. On the very crest of the barranca could be seen, through glasses, man-made walls of stone. This was the fortified site of Chutixtiox and it deserved the word fortified most definitely from this side.

"We circle around to the north," Ted explained, "and there we cross a bridge and approach the ruin by a gradual slope."

We lost altitude until we came to the village of Sacapulas. In the small plaza was an enormous jacaranda tree whose inviting shade asked us to use the spot for lunch.

Ledyard disappeared and returned with bottles of warm beer. Our hotel-prepared lunches were opened without the least hope of discovering surprises. The hard-boiled egg, the chicken sandwich, the orange, were all there.

The hungry dogs, the shy children, soon formed their silent circle and we lunched *como siempre* in the Highlands. Hastily we swallowed the fare and headed for the path leading up the long slope to the ruins.

Soon we were climbing over low, eroded walls, part of the ancient fortification on that side where nature had provided none.

It was a hot, humid noonday and already I faced the first obstacle to acceptance of this site: how could we ever get tourists here? There was no road, and building one within our budget was impossible. Even a quantity of burros would only partially overcome the discomfort of the average sightseer, should he straddle one.

But a challenging picture it was, once we had arrived at the top and stood in the main plaza. A quadrangle of buildings, some temple-like, others with remains of rooms, surrounded the plaza. Restoration definitely would have been a challenge but one that would reward us handsomely. Most of the fallen stone was within easy reach.

Ledyard Smith had always yearned to dig this remote ninth century ruin. He had every justification for pressing it upon me as the one we should select. From then on I detected a lessening of interest in other sites and a relaxation of his participation as a consultant, and I could not blame him. In his honest opinion, commercial aspects of archaeology were outcast. His background was a puritanical one which encompassed financing of such affairs purely by scientific organizations; no commercial participation belonged in his vocation.

Reluctantly, we left Chutixtiox and continued up the river to its main source, and the ruins of Chalchitan. Here the mysterious source of the Rio Negro surges out of the mountain in a volume unbelievable and spreads its waters over an oasis.

We sat on the low banks of the stream, our bare feet, hot from the day of exploring, dangling in the cool waters, and gazed at the verdant acres on every side.

Vegetables grow in even rows, but onions, watercress and garlic prevail. This is still one of the delightful waypoints of all Guatemala and shamefully overlooked. I would have seriously considered this ruin but my advisors pointed out the fault: the buildings had been systematically robbed of stone for many years. We left reluctantly.

That night, reeking of garlic and onions, we arrived in Huehuetenango to find that this was dance night at the hotel and the marimba band would be on hand.

Marimba dances are command performances; it is impossible to sleep until the music, steadily losing cadence but gathering volume, finally ceases. So it is far easier to attend than to lie awake cursing it. But tomorrow we were to be off for Zaculeu, the site which, though none of us knew it at the moment, would end our search.

Huehuetenango itself had charm. The two small hotels were not the postcard-to-home type, but were adequate, clean, and the food passable. The Huehuetenango market was large and active. It held forth in the ruins of some early buildings and was open every day. The square and its church lent color and formed the gathering area for the populace in the evening. Father Allié the priest and Brother Felix were to become our fast friends.

Next morning we drove a bit less than three miles to the ruins of Zaculeu. We stopped momentarily on an eroded segment of the road leading down to the ruins. From there the chronicle of battle, skirmishes and capture of the city by the Spanish could be vividly imagined. Our final report on the ruins, written three years later, contained an excellent history of Zaculeu by Nathalie Woodbury, wife of Richard Woodbury, our archaeologist for the final two years. I have borrowed in part from the research and resultant account compiled so well by Nathalie to describe the overthrow and subjugation of the fortified city.

SINCE THE YEAR 1521, when Cortez had commissioned the Alvarados, Pedro and Gonzalo, to conquer and control the lands now known as Guatemala and Salvador, the brothers had left a trail of murder, enslavement and wreckage throughout those coastal areas and had embarked upon the conquest of the Highlands. The tough resistance of the Quiche had been broken and their numbers either decimated or enlisted.

In the fall of 1525 Gonzalo and his forces entered Huehuetenango, already deserted by its Mam Indian inhabitants and their leader, Caibil Balam.

Balam had retreated to the fortified city of Zaculeu, entering it no doubt within a few yards of where we now stood, through a gate in the east wall. All other sides were protected by nature in the form of a deep and precipitous ravine that would successfully deny approach to either foot soldiers or cavalry.

Alvarado's forces had made themselves comfortable in Huehuetenango and were ready to reconnoitre the situation at Zaculeu. Caibil Balam knew that he and his small force were next on the military program of Alvarado. Having sealed himself within the Zaculeu complex, he placed some 300 Mam archers in the field between himself and the enemy at Huehuetenango.

There was little fight in those men, however, and when they were attacked by only ten horsemen they retreated, leaving seven dead and three captured. The captured told the Spanish that Balam was inside the fortress of Zaculeu with his entire court and that his plan was simply to stay there until the white strangers had departed. He would depend upon his friends from the outside of the fort to supply him food and water.

Alvarado did not relish the idea of a direct attack on Zaculeu. He attempted to persuade Caibil Balam to surrender without combat, explaining that his purposes were peaceful, for spreading the Christian faith. He, at the same time, threatened Caibil Balam with death and destruction should he fail to capitulate. Balam made no reply whatsoever and after three days Alvarado again sent word but his messengers were fired upon with arrows by the defenders.

Furious at this lack of respect, Alvarado marched immediately on Zaculeu. The Spanish and Mam forces joined battle on the east side of the fortress. Although outnumbered as much as ten to one the Spanish, with their cavalry and superior weapons, soon turned the battle into a debacle for the Mam. Several hundred were killed by the first charge and the balance retreated in disorder. Those who were able rushed through the gates of the fortress and barricaded themselves inside. The Spanish had lost some forty Indian recruits and three horses. Gonzalo himself was slightly wounded, as was his brother Francisco, who had joined his forces. (Pedro was not at Zaculeu.)

Gonzalo de Alvarado dispersed his troops around the fortress and the siege of Zaculeu had begun. He established his own headquarters just outside the gate where he was prepared to direct the attack on the Mam or wait out their surrender. At one point the Spanish attempted to build an access road on the west side of the city, a hazardous undertaking since it had to be cut into an almost vertical face.

However, the job was progressing slowly even under constant harassment and attack by the defenders, when word came that some eight thousand supporters of the Mam were coming across the plains from the north. These hopeful rescuers had come down from the mountains in full war paint and regalia, armed with lances and arrows. Gonzalo de Alvarado's contempt for those besieged within was emphasized by his leaving only ten Spaniards and some five hundred Quiche and other Indians to guard the gate while he marshalled the balance of his forces to meet the approaching enemy. The new attackers were not bad soldiers and were skilled in the use of their weapons. But the Spanish again were protected by their heavily quilted coats while the Mam Indians had no protection from the crossbow and harquebus. At the given moment, the rescuers were routed in disorder by the cavalry. All of this was most discouraging to Caibil Balam. He attempted a night escape along with a few of his trusted lieutenants. No doubt he had hopes that if he could reach the mountains where his allies were, he could reform the army under his own leadership. His escape try was a failure and he was forced to retreat, slightly wounded, back to the fortress.

The Spanish also were unhappy with the progress of the siege. Food was running low, to the point where the Indian troops were eating the dead horses which had fallen in battle. But the temporary famine of the Spanish was certain to be assuaged. Eventually, they were supplied from their sources to the south with beans, fowl and deer meat, and they were fully prepared to outlast Caibil Balam. Indian smugglers were killed when captured and the food intended for the besieged went to the besiegers.

Both sides were suffering severely from the chills and rain of late October. In desperation and anger, Gonzalo decided to make an attack on all fronts. The Mam losses up to that time were already staggering, both from starvation and from constant sniping attacks. Nothing could be grown within the fortress for foodstuffs. There was no meat except for the ghastly possibility of eating their own dead, a probability but never a proven certainty.

After three days of deliberation, Balam decided to ask for a truce. The surrender accomplished, he and a dozen or so of his men came forward. He was overcome with emotion when he understood that Gonzalo really intended to treat him with kindness, only admonishing him for not surrendering in the first place and avoiding the terrible loss of life.

The Mam fortress of Zaculeu was formally taken over by the Spanish. The gate was destroyed, and after establishing a garrison in Huehuetenango, Alvarado decided that any further conquest of the north country was unnecessary and he returned in triumph to Guatemala City.

We continued our approach along the inclined road and through what remained of the stone gate and entered the main plaza of Zaculeu.

The history of this Highland Maya city was fairly well documented from the time of the Spanish conquest. Beneath those ruins lay bits of the pre-Columbian story we were after.

Instantly, the compact ruin convinced me that we had reached our goal. It had everything required for our program. Its grass-covered mounds were still high enough to assure sufficient evidence beneath for authentic restoration. Its principal temple structure was seventy feet high and in first class condition. The setting of the ruin was one that visitors from afar would remember always. It was surrounded by a deep gully except for the small neck supporting the entrance road. Also, although these features should and did rank second, it had what was so vital to my decision: the city of Huehuetenango within three miles where we could live, get supplies and find labor; ample water from the small river at its base for making concrete and adobe; and, highly convincing, an airstrip only two miles away where a plane landed weekly from Guatemala City. (After our first season's work, the traffic to and from Huehuetenango became so demanding that we had three planes a week.)

These factors were pertinent, vital to the success of our program. After discussion with Ted Kidder, I made the decision that, with permission of the Fruit Company, we would accept this site in preference to Chutixtiox. That afternoon we called on the mayor of Huehuetenango and told him of our plans and hopes. We encountered nothing but enthusiastic approval from him. Visions of employment and local trade settled all doubt as to his reactions. Every day now that held up the start would put us further into the important dry season which was soon to begin. We were ready to return to Guatemala City.

On the way back, I was enthusiastic but not happy. I was beginning to understand these two fine men in the car with me.

The selection would have been otherwise had they been making it. Zaculeu had been quarried in places for stone to build Huehuetenango. It had been visited by John L. Stephens, the intrepid explorer of Central America, in the early nineteenth century and thus was not the untouched or unpublished monument that was Chutixtiox.

But most painful, here were two men who had been working for years in remote places on small budgets, living often in the crudest fashion conceivable for a white man. How could they be expected to embrace enthusiastically my selection which had been made, in their opinion, principally for its creature comforts, for the diggers and the expected visitors. I knew my boss and what he would expect from his investment, and justly so. The Fruit Company would accept Zaculeu, and would not approve Chutixtiox.

In 1938 in Salvador, I had learned a bitter lesson: a Bit Player simply cannot, just by his own desires and ambitions, become the Heavy. There was more to archaeology than making a map, digging a few holes, and recovering objects. Now that I had my funds and my site, the all important next step was recruiting a skilled crew. During the time of my distress in Salvador, when I attempted to excavate a beautiful ceremonial site alone and was rapidly coming to grief, I appealed to Ted Kidder in Guatemala City. Ted had a young man available who had worked with Carnegie before, Stanley Boggs. I liked Stan and when Ted Kidder told me he was available for Zaculeu, I was delighted. We contacted Boggs and he agreed to come, along with his Salvadorian wife. I relished the prospect of having a Latin American matron around. She could, if she would, take over housekeeping.

I spent days at the new museum in Guatemala City, examining artifacts and pottery and endeavoring to ingratiate myself with the museum heads who would pass upon our production at Zaculeu. The Guatemalan Museum had agreed on the site we had chosen without question or suggestion of alternative. The men themselves were socially polite. Yet there was something indefinable, some feeling within me that all was not as it should be. Finally the answer trickled through to me. I was the cause of their reserve. I, the dilettante, with no background, no experience and certainly no reputation. Yet here I was director of the project. The fact that Stanley Boggs had a long record of worthy performance in Latin American archaeology did not ameliorate the uncertain feelings of these men appointed to guard the antiquities of their country.

When the solution came to me it was difficult to understand how, in my anxiety and haste to commence operations, I had overlooked such a simple answer: Ted Kidder, with a quarter century of experience in Latin American archaeology, who was beloved and respected throughout the country, not only in his field but for his lofty moral standards and his affection for Guatemala itself. I would ask the Fruit Company to appoint Kidder its representative for inspection of the work at Zaculeu and give him full control over our methods of research and restoration.

In quick order I had the Company's approval of the plan and Kidder's reluctant but final agreement to act. "Ted," I begged, "we have gone this far, do this for me and the project." I used persuasions best known to him, that I had no background, couldn't parley as he could with the government bigwigs. "They need only look into their own Museum to realize what you have done for them." Time would approve this fortunate alliance.

Stan and Nee Boggs departed for Huehuetenango while I remained in the City to purchase our many needs, available only there. Boggs lost no time in locating two houses on a little street leading off the Plaza. One, he said, would serve as an office, drafting area and collection space for our finds. It had also a large patio where we could take advantage of the sunlight for our photography and repair work. In addition, it would provide a safe area for storing large artifacts.

Across the street was a little adobe house which would suffice for the Boggs family. Both were within a few minutes of the main square and markets. I was to put up in the best local hotel.

Boggs brought with him Daniel Murcia, a Honduranian lad who had worked with him as foreman at Copan. Daniel was a lucky find. Not only did he understand and know how to handle the native Indian workmen but he was an expert in pottery mending. He developed into an indispensable asset.

My purchases in the city included canned food, beds, mattresses, blankets, linens, cooking utensils and china. Our station wagon was ready for travel and loaded with my stocks. I was off on my first unaccompanied trek into the highlands. My inadequate Spanish was no hindrance and after two days of leisurely travel, I arrived in Huehuetenango.

Boggs had accomplished wonders in the few days he had been there. Carpenters were busy building work tables, cabinets, benches and hard chairs. He had found some tubular lights and was having them strung along the ceilings of our dingy workrooms. They swung precariously by wire, their luminescence varying with the power furnished by Huehuetenango's whimsical and only generator. Our bright new shovels, hoes, trowels, wheelbarrows, and machetes were on hand, as was our surveying equipment. Murcia had recruited our first labor group from farmers near the site. The labor well was overflowing and we turned men away with sincere promises that, when transportation from Huehuetenango was available, we would take them on in the order of their application.

Daniel had reconnoitered the site and had found a deserted adobe shack. He made a door for it with padlock and that became our warehouse for storage of tools at night. We were ready to begin...

One lone farmer, Manuel, and his family lived at the ruins. He was happy to become our night watchman and we soon learned

ZACULEU *Restoration of the terraces was under way while we explored the center lines of Temple I. A small dancing platform is in foreground.*

Temple IV as found.

Temple IV restored, with right wing cleaned but unrestored. Compare with partially restored wing at left.

Above: An excellent example of architectural technique in archaeology—a wall had fallen in its entirety, probably from an earthquake, then became covered by centuries of windblown earth. The archaeologist uncovered, found its base, and erected it as it originally stood.

Right: Zaculeu has been relentlessly robbed of stone for many years for modern building. For reconstruction we cast 300 cement blocks a day by hand. Sheds were erected to prevent rapid drying.

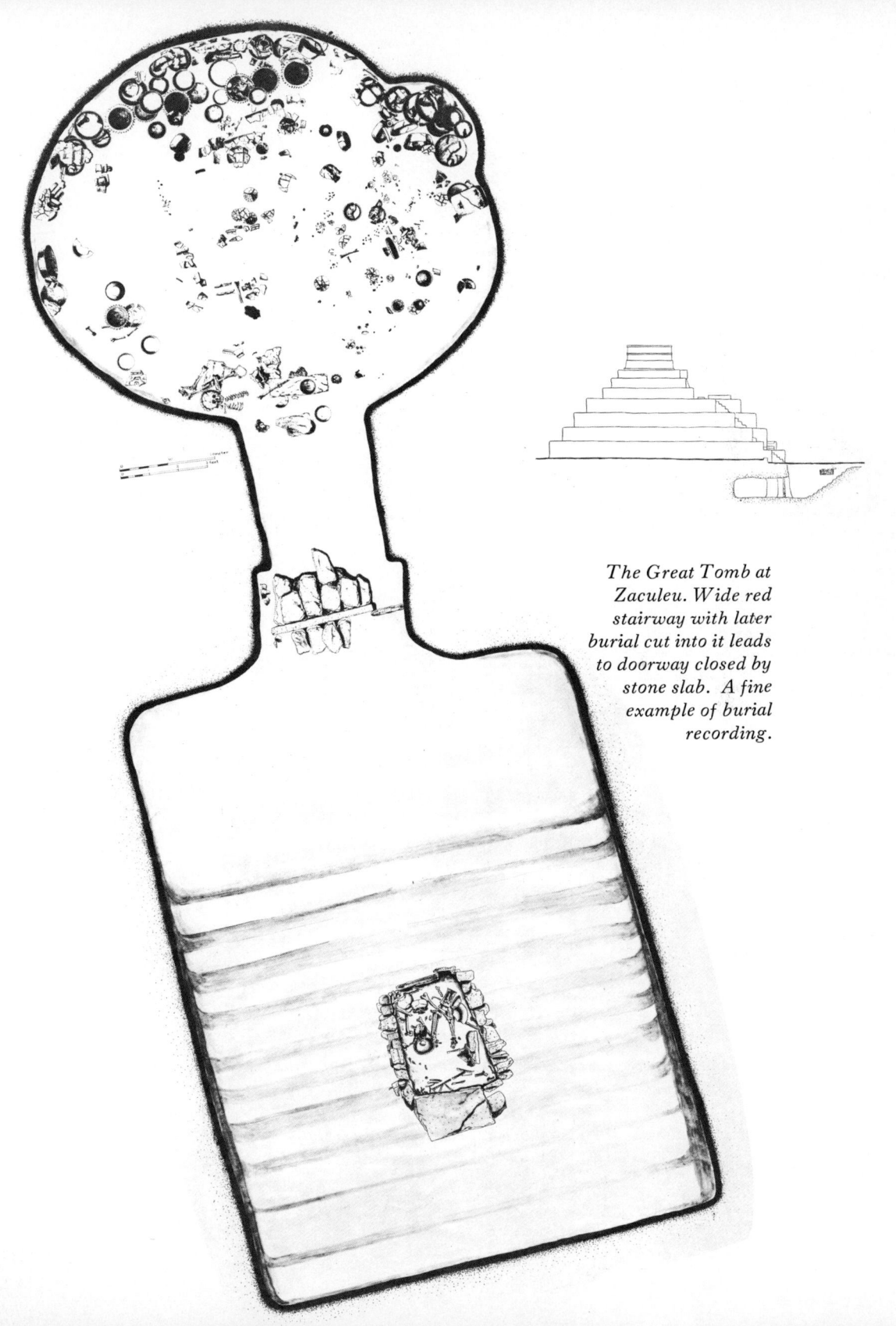

The Great Tomb at Zaculeu. Wide red stairway with later burial cut into it leads to doorway closed by stone slab. A fine example of burial recording.

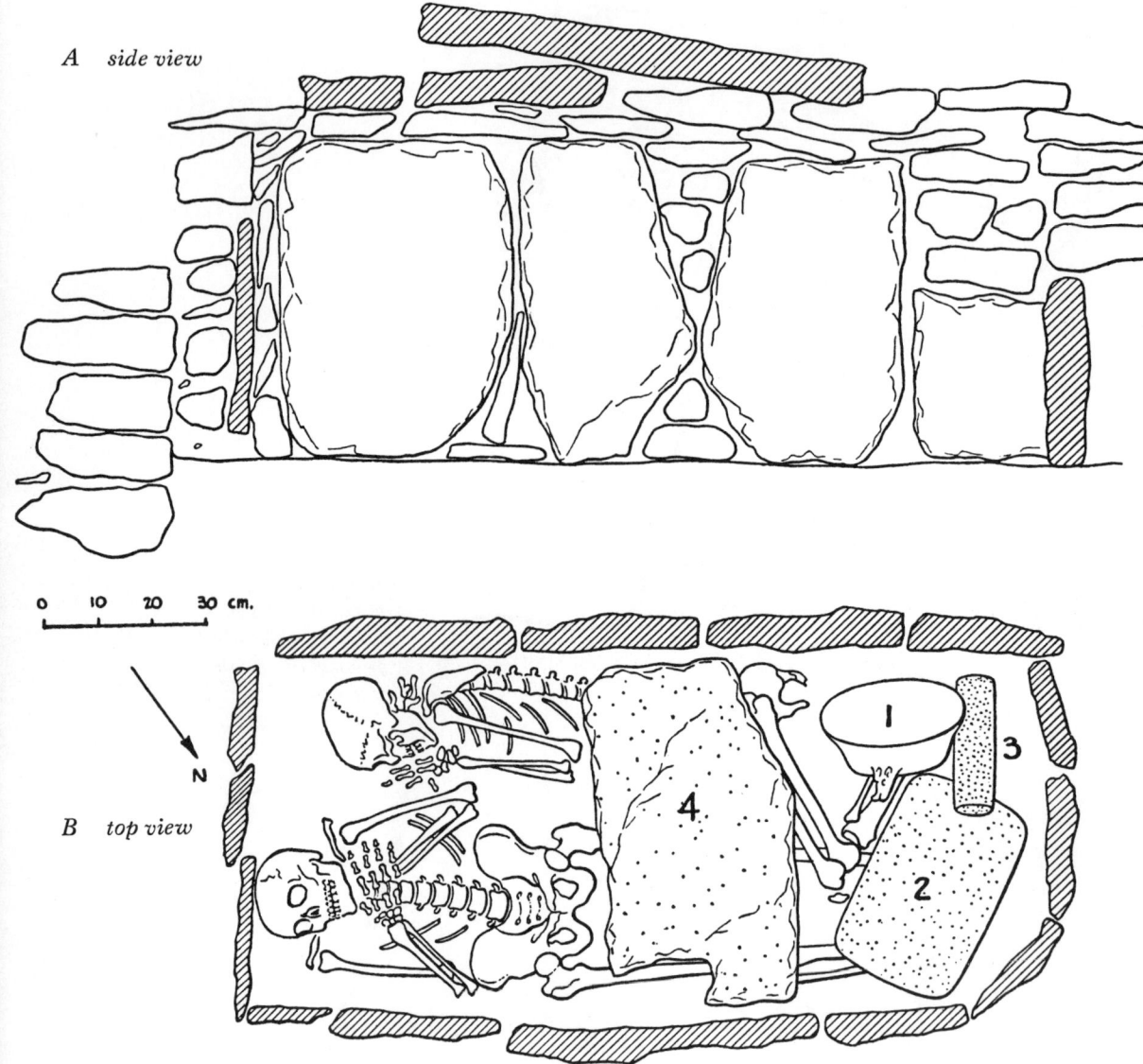

Details of graves are recorded by accurate field measurements which in turn are executed into drawings.
A Elevation of one side of a grave.
B Plan of same burial discloses two persons partially covered by a random stone (4), a bowl (1), and a grinding metate (2) with roller (3).

An example of meticulous cleaning by the archaeologist discloses a typical multiple burial at Zaculeu. Four skulls and scattered skeletal material indicate mass interment.

Left: Cautious digging and careful recording discloses intricate mass burial at Zaculeu: the smashed lid of an urn with only the skull showing.

Above: The urn cleaned down to its base, ladle and incensario uncovered

Right: Gradually the entire grave complex is disclosed, exposing four burials

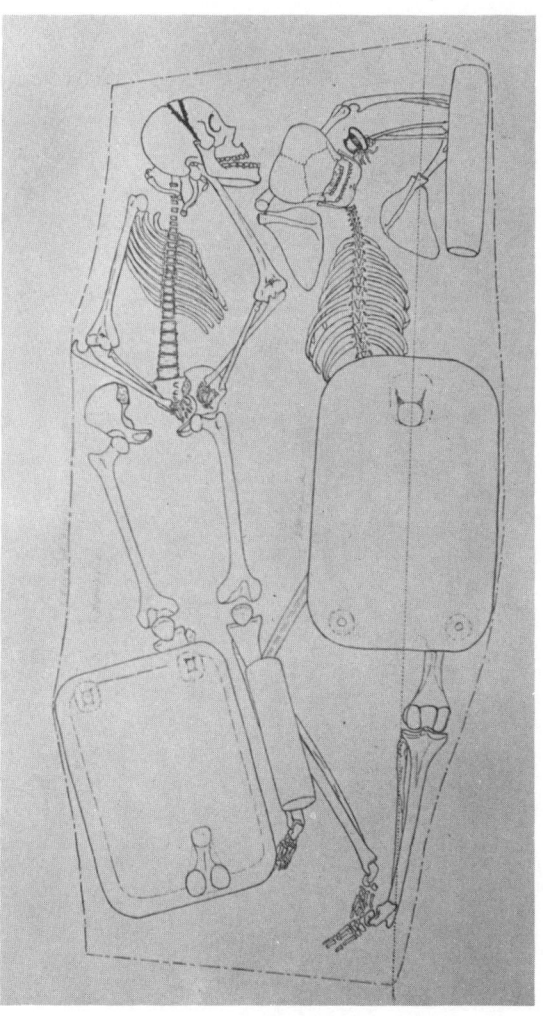

This double burial could have been of two servants, each with a tripodal metate and mano for making corn meal.

Typical prone and intact burials offered the digger his best opportunity for skeletal measurements and diagnosis of infirmities, causes of death and age of the deceased.

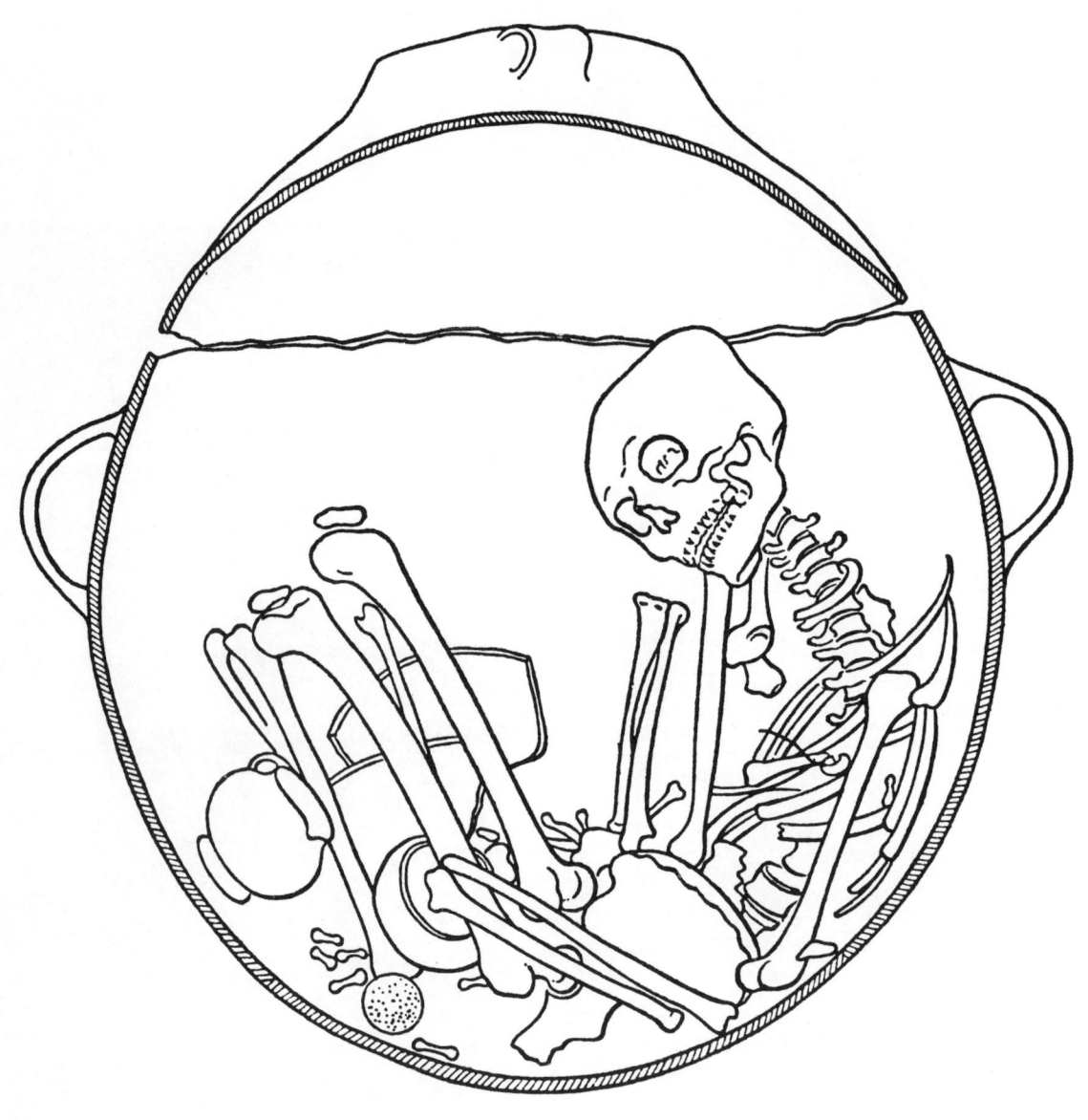

Measured drawing of urn burial in the Museum at Zaculeu.

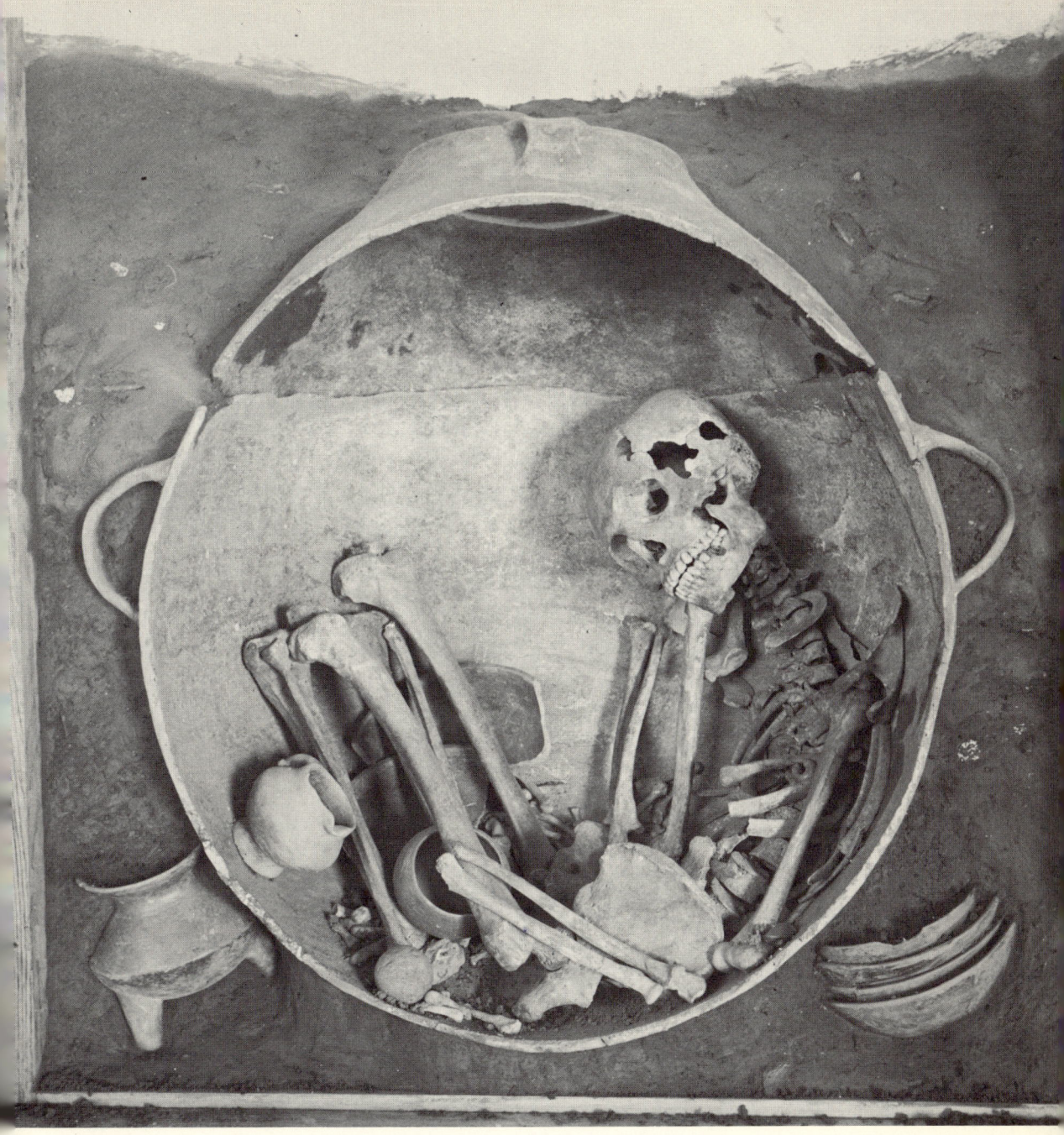

Photograph of same burial as found.

Top: Ball court as found. Note white floor which is evident in a few places.

Bottom: After grubbing and cleaning, the sloping sides and corners appear.

After lines and corners are established, restoration is begun. However, restoration is not carried beyond the point of positive proof.

Left: Finishing touches are added to the restoration.

Below and opposite page: Views of the completed Ball Court.

Entire classes visited the ruins and were treated to lecture tours.

that he had become a self-appointed guide as well, explaining in his own fashion just what was happening when native visitors came to the ruins after we departed for the day. His fantastic stories became embarassing to refute and eventually we quit trying.

Boggs and Nee had their meals with me at the hotel until Nee had arranged a kitchen and a water supply in their little hut. Their presence at mealtime helped with my Spanish but they found it difficult to restrain my talking. One night the mayor of the city was dining at the hotel. He finished ahead of us and with the usual Spanish custom as he passed the table he politely said "Buen provecho," or good appetite. Not to be outdone and before Stanley could stop me, I retorted "Gracios adios," certain I had said "Thanks and goodbye." Idiomatically I had said "Thank God you're gone." The mayor gave me a very hard look then realized what had happened. Whereupon he did not just smile, he burst into laughter, the most belittling slap he could possibly have administered.

We were supplied with adequate lunches by the hotel and, after early breakfast, we would arrive on the site at about seven. The first week was spent in grubbing the ruins and laying out our base lines for the survey of buildings. A general plan of procedure included first the cutting into one of the smaller structures with a trench through its centerline. Once we had started trenching, we realized that wheelbarrows would never accommodate the enormous amount of earth to be moved away from the cut. Furthermore all, or most of it, had to be returned some day when the exploration was completed and the restoration was at hand. A dump truck became a necessity, something I had not included in the budget. *Gracias Dios* for my built-in safety factor for funds. Equal obeisance to my sponsor, the United Fruit Company, whose weekly ships from New York assured us of quick delivery of the truck. We could have the truck by New Year's, the beginning of the second half of the season.

In the meantime, the Public Relations section of UFCO had lost no time in announcing the project and telling those making excursions on the Great White Fleet that they would have the opportunity to see Zaculeu as a part of their tour to the Highlands of Guatemala. E. S. Whitman, Vice President of United Fruit in charge of Public Relations became my invaluable friend. Before the end of that half-season, tourists were coming in busloads and by private car. Entire classrooms of Guatemalan students were brought by their teachers in buses, picnicking on the grounds, racing to the tops of temples. People came in such quantities that it was necessary to hire and train guides to answer the myriad questions and to escort them properly through the ruins.

We endeavored to instruct the guides and chauffeurs, in order to give them a true picture. However, the story we gave was not sufficiently exciting to their manner of thinking, and in no time we overheard them telling the most fantastic stories of the pre-Columbian Indian, purely inventions of their own fancy.

Our carefully cut sidewalls of trenches and tombs were no barrier to those avid onlookers. Each one insisted upon standing on the very edge of the work area and as a consequence a crypt or a burial, having just been carefully cleaned for measuring or photographing, would suddenly be immersed in fine dust, with nothing more remedial than "Oh I'm so sorry!" from above. Rope lines had to be installed around the work areas in some cases. Who knows if all of us possess a measure of ghoulishness or if it is agitated by the site of interments exposed with all their decorative pots and jades? One morning, we were cleaning a beautifully preserved skeleton in what is called a prone burial. It was surrounded by some extremely fine pottery. We were replete with visitors that morning, mostly that easily defined type of middle-aged lady whose husband had either passed away leaving her alone but well financed for travel, or who has remained at home to provide. The job of cleaning was slow, removing the encrustation from the bones tedious. The ladies were surrounding the tomb, gleefully discussing the unfortunate fellow within who had obviously been dealt a mortal skull blow. They were glued to that one spot, caring nothing for the organized tour which was in progress. Finally, one poor woman could stand it no longer. She leaned far over where she could see the meticulous cleaning job going on and shouted, "For God's sake, lift him out where we can look at him, we can't stay here all day!"

    As the work progressed towards the end of the first season and more of the building surfaces were revealed, we realized that originally they were pure glistening white. Semblances of vari-colored paint showed in places but the base color in all cases was white. In order to positively confirm the surface finish and to be assured of accomplishing an authentic restoration, we carefully cleaned areas of numerous buildings in the complex. All were definitely pure white and still maintained, where they had been protected by earth for centuries, a glossiness comparable to the inside of a bathtub.
    The Indians had employed white lime to face their temples, and when that surface became worn or dirty, or they wished to change the shape slightly, they simply added another coat. That method, of course, we could not follow. We had to rebuild for perpetuity and that meant we must employ white cement. I shuddered to guess at the amount of that commodity we would require and where it would come from and at what cost. But here again the Fruit Company came to our rescue. There were two thousand bags of white cement from Yugoslavia lying at the Company's operation on the west coast of Guatemala. It was sent to us by truck along with a monstrous bill of lading which during the three years of work we forgot to pay.
    Somehow we had struggled through the first half-season until Christmas time without Aubrey Trik. Looking back upon it, and in spite of the yeoman's job done by Boggs in excava-

tion, I realize the injection of skill and general know-how Aubrey added to the job, once he had arrived. I can't think what our final result would have been without him.

Trik was another "find" of Ted Kidder. He was an architect, just back from sea duty in the Pacific at the war's end. He had been on the staff of Carnegie Institution during the excavations and preservation of the huge city of Copan in Honduras, an early Maya site. Among other accomplishments he had done an excellent job in recording one of the complex temples there. He wanted to get back into archaeology and Kidder recommended him to take charge of our architectural recording, burials and restoration. Kidder's words in favor of Aubrey turned out to be one of his better understatements. Trik arrived after Christmas that first year.

In the meantime Boggs had decided that he wanted time in the United States, where his family owned a large Indiana farm. He left us after doing some highly commendable archaeological work, and a rising young archaeologist, Richard Woodbury came in his stead. Woodbury is now curator of North American Anthropology at The Smithsonian Institution. From the first, this was a fine combination, Trik and Woodbury. Each was excellent in his own field, Woodbury with his skill in ceramics and general finds, and Trik with his background of architecture and construction. High gear was achieved with that combination. The bit player could relax in the wings and enjoy the performance.

The dear old matron of our little hotel was at first overjoyed at the sudden boom in her business brought on by the tourist influx. But the job was too much for her. She simply could not think and act in terms of such numbers. Food became a problem both in quantity and quality. Service deteriorated. Then appeared a man who agreed to buy her out and that man was one John Smith.

This story would be sadly incomplete without the saga of John and his stay in Huehuetenango. At about the turn of the century, John's Texas father and mother had brought him and four other children, of which he was the eldest, across the mountains from Mexico into Guatemala along with a herd of smuggled cattle. John was only ten when he watched his father kill his first Indian, one of a gang which tried to murder them all. John himself was wielding a rifle before that perilous crossing was finished. The family settled on the western plains of Guatemala at a time when every man was his own protector. Cattle were coveted and remained with the strong. After his father's death, John was head of the family. All learned Spanish by necessity.

When Guatemala came under its first important dictator, Ubico, the boys had grown into men, hard driving, bilingual men who had learned to trade ruthlessly, but honestly when possible. They entered into many ventures, importing, retailing, then hotels. John saw the possibilities of a hotel at Huehuetenango and thereby hangs the story of our acquaintance.

Trik and I spent that first half-season with John, watching him develop the rundown hotel into a clean, well-managed little hostelry where we were not only comfortable but happy. This friendship became far more valuable to us as we progressed. John knew how to trade with the Indians, what was a fair price for whatever we needed. The natives trusted him and most important, would deliver when he demanded.

John opened a small bar in the hotel where we were his only patrons other than tourists. He could not enjoy an evening drink with us unless we agreed to roll the dice for it, and he lost far more times than he won.

When Trik and I decided that we really did need a house of our own, it was John who found it for us, dickered with the owner on the rent and helped us acquire the necessary materials which could be found locally. (At the end of the work at Zaculeu two years thence when we were laden with equipment which was not worth moving, it was John who bought it all in situ.) He used some of our photographs and produced his own brochure to advertise the ruins as a place to visit, and see archaeology in progress. He even got us memberships to the Bath and Tennis Club of Huehuetenango (no baths and no tennis, but it did have a bar and a passably good billiard table, the social spot of the town.) The fact that John is not mentioned in our coldly factual, two-volume report on Zaculeu is mute testimony to the lackluster of such publications.

We had made good headway in that first half-season under Boggs, who rightly decided that we should not attack the trench into the large temple structure until we were prepared to make the architectural drawing as the work progressed. Boggs trenched some of the smaller buildings along their centerlines and came up with numbers of graves and burials, enough to convince us that the Maya had interred a number of their people within the precincts of the site, not in some outlying area which we might search for vainly.

Pottery and other objects commenced to accumulate in large quantities. The work rooms and the patio in our small house in Huehuetenango were put to the uses we had planned for them, recording the finds and repairing the pottery.

After the first of the year when Trik arrived, and later Richard Woodbury, we had the power to attack the ruin in full force and record its secrets. Trik laid out a six-foot-wide trench leading into the large temple platform from about fifty feet out.

No sooner had we begun digging there than we had evidence of things to come. We had barely reached the bottom edge of the temple when our first burial appeared, only a few feet below the surface. The grave itself was not an exciting one. It consisted of a large urn, badly broken. It contained one skeleton (an adult female according to Trik).

That was a type of burial we were to encounter often. The Indians had cut the large urn just above the center. They would double the body into a sort of sitting position and place it within the lower part of the urn, along with selected gifts of jewels, small pots and other of their treasures, then replace the top and bury the entire urn. Not a bad preservation method, far more permanent than many of the rock tombs we were to find caved-in directly upon the unfortunate occupants.

When we had cleaned that grave and proceeded towards the great temple wall, Trik suddenly came upon a vivid red color in the solid earth. Moving cautiously, he soon discovered that he was unearthing a red-painted step. It had to be first evidence of something large and important to come.

Three steps lower we reached a second burial. The vault-like affair was in loose fill above the stairway, not cut into the natural earth as had been the one before. Therefore, its sidewalls were constructed to stand on their own. Well-cut stone slabs placed vertically formed the ends. Horizontal stones laid in mud formed the sides.

Inside was such a melange of skulls and bones that Trik and Woodbury agreed that it had been reused, at least once, possibly more often, without proper interval cleaning. Its contents were disappointing and we quickly recorded it and continued down the stairway. Twelve of these red steps in all took us to a floor some fifteen feet below the plaza surface. After a foot or so of horizontal clearing, there was the great red door!

It matters little if one is Sir Arthur Evans at Knossos or Howard Carter at the tomb of Tutankhamen, the electrifying thrill of a tomb door never wanes. For us, this first evidence of something delectable to come was overwhelming. We had found our big tomb beneath the temple. The door was about five feet high and some three feet across. It was a well-cut slab more than four inches thick, braced at the bottom with small stones and canted just enough to hold it in place. Impatience had to be restrained until we had cleaned, measured and photographed the slab in place.

Finally, all scholarly matters attended to, we were ready to move that huge red barrier and have our first look within. Lifting the door was no easy task. A scaffold and blocks and tackle were set in place and gradually the ponderous slab was hoisted to the surface. One constantly wonders, using modern gear in the research of ruins, how the aborigines who originated the work, having nothing but their own puissance, accomplished their many miracles of heft.

The stone safely above, we flashed our torches into the dark unknown space before us. No one knows what to expect when faced with such an adventure. Our first reaction was to the vastness of the area as compared with tombs we had seen and read of, in the Highlands. From the door we could not accurately estimate the distance to the back wall.

Inevitably such huge burial chambers, when dug into the earth below a temple structure, have caved in. Timbers supporting the roof decay and crumble from weight and earthquakes bring down upon the remains suffocating amounts of earth and debris.

Our tomb was no exception. The floor was covered with debris to the point that we could not guess how far below it was. This was the first major tomb I had ever seen untouched by modern man. All the promotion and the effort and the waiting of the past year were rewarded in that one sight.

Everything halted until we had brought and installed necessary lighting. Kerosene lights were found in Huehuetenango and placed near the entrance. Then began the slow and tedious job of clearing away the fallen debris and searching for the tomb bed.

Trik performed like the skilled technician he was known to be as he approached the tomb floor, some 12 feet in diameter. Methodically he cleaned, recorded and drew every object in place.

In no time, word reached Huehuetenango that we had a spectacular discovery. During the day sightseers came in increasing, inquisitive numbers. During the night we posted guards to prevent entry. After several days of backbreaking work, with the help of a native who had been trained by Trik, we reached the level where we could expect the tomb treasures, if there were to be treasures. So often those enormous and perfectly located chambers had already been looted, either by earlier diggers or more often by the very Indians themselves, shortly after interment. But we were not to be foiled in this one. Skeletal material came to light at the entrance and continued to the tomb center. Trik has stated in the Zaculeu report that there were at least seven persons buried there. But the remains were so disintegrated that it was impossible in some cases to tell exactly how the bodies had been arranged. Two young children had been placed near the entrance, while across the entrance were two adult skeletons which Trik decided were guards placed there to protect the royal occupants through eternity. That conclusion in my opinion was a sound one, based on the disclosure that these two skeletons were the only ones in the group which had no artifacts or gifts of any nature associated with their bodies, thus relegating them to the level of servitude.

The center of the tomb was almost bare, except for the skeletal material and some minor adornments which had no doubt been part of the bedecking of the bodies when placed there. But when we reached the periphery of the tomb, against its walls we found the real storehouse of treasure. Over a hundred pots, jades and stone objects were huddled against the walls, in disarray now, but no doubt lovingly placed more than a thousand years before.

There were jade mosaic pieces, shell beads, decorated jade beads, and ear plugs. There were effigy pendants in jade, quartz crystal ornaments, literally dozens of beautiful bowls, incense burners, conch shell trumpets. There were mirrors of pyrites, even the skull of an ocelot. We gathered every possible box and crate we could find in Huehuetenango, filled them with sand or shavings, and gingerly packed our discoveries into them,—making many slow trips in the station wagon before we had transferred everything to the office. During the next two years, we were to open many graves at Zaculeu but our climax had come early in this lucrative tomb, the only one of its kind discovered there. Possibly there are others in some of the buildings we did not explore completely.

We seriously considered keeping the tomb as an exhibit, leaving it open and installing a permanent stairway so that visitors could see the entire layout. But good sense prevailed and the fear of a cave-in brought on by some future earthquake influenced our decision to fill the huge molehole we had dug and close it forever.

Of the many achievements which mark the pandiculation of archaeology during the past quarter century, nothing in my opinion is so pronounced as the ingenuity to preserve the ruins as an integral part of the entire project, an articulated feature of the planning from the beginning. For too long, the reckless objective was to unearth the treasures, desecrating the buildings in the search for loot to adorn museum shelves and private collections throughout the world. Many ancient Latin American ruins are mute evidence of this sort of vandalism carried on in the early and mid years of the nineteenth century and continued in petty fashion for profit right up to the present.

There was no question from the start of our program at Zaculeu that the ruins would be carefully preserved where it could be done authentically, and that our explorative trenches would be filled and the building structures replaced to our best ability with durable materials to protect them from the heavy rains, erosion and earthquakes.

The aboriginal builders of Zaculeu had brought lime from the high valley to the east and produced their white mortar in prodigious quantities. Adobe mud, reinforced with random broken stone, was used for basic fill. The lime plaster was then carefully troweled over the rough surfaces to produce the smooth white finishes. We negotiated with the Indians, descendants no doubt of those early men who had packed the lime rock on their backs down from the hills, to deliver lime to us. The "modern" Indians now had small burros which could carry two hundred pounds each, carefully divided into equal weights on each side.

We agreed on a price per hundred pounds, which set the delivery into motion. One small breach of contract occurred and recurred until our foreman, Daniel Murcia, caught up with it. It was easier at times to just drop in a few boulders to make up the weight. But a drop in our purchase price by Daniel soon improved the purity of our product.

The lime was dumped in the plaza where it was smashed by sledge hammers and arranged in large disc-shaped piles. It was then thoroughly soaked with water and quickly began to bubble and boil. Soon we had ample mortar for our fill, but where were we to find the stone? It was not available for miles and would have to be quarried, wherever we found it. I contacted the Fruit Company for cement and as usual it came to hand. We had come up with the solution. We could make concrete blocks. After all, we had the river sand and water. We were able to buy two forms. In a few days we were turning out from a hundred to a hundred and fifty blocks per day.

Our water delivery before the truck came was difficult but amusing. Poles were rigged for cross-shoulder carrying and a five gallon can put at each end. Each man sent to the river with his gear was expected to bring back at least a fair percentage of water to be poured into our five or six fifty-gallon steel gasoline drums. But it was a long tiresome struggle up the hill with ten gallons of water and the trips became fewer and the can contents less as the day went on. Again a simple solution was found: We gave notice to the carriers that when the drums were filled, regardless of the time of day, they could go off with a full day's pay. From then on the drums were brimming full by shortly after lunch. That expediency was no longer necessary once United Fruit sent our dump truck. The drums were then loaded on the truck, filled by hand by our barefoot men wading in the river, and brought to the plaza. However, when time came for mixing and applying our white cement, along with the puddling and mixing of adobe and lime, water supply again became our worry.

The cry again went to the Company, and again it was answered in the form of a hundred-barrel steel tank. We built a low platform for it, in order to create enough gravity, bolted the plates into shape and mounted it. Now we began to look like a full-fledged construction outfit.

Zaculeu in its position contrives a harmonious communion with nature, like a jeweled setting. The impression today differs but little from five hundred years ago. The spaced white buildings, over a mile above sea level, form a cluster against the broad breast of the Cuchumatanes mountains which rise an additional four thousand feet to the north. To complete the complex, the jade-colored Selegua river circles the steep-sided platform to the west and south.

Frequently during the dry season, from November until April, the ruins were shrouded by heavy fog in early morning, leaving only the tips of the buildings standing above the mist like small limestone islands. The sun quickly dissipated the fog; a blanket of light dew lay on the ground, and in turn gave way to the increasing temperature. Sweaters were soon discarded and just a sleeveless khaki shirt was ample.

The winds came with the rising sun, often increasing to a state of discomfort. Lifted shovels loaded with dirt from the excavations left a dust plume trailing from their tips before they could be emptied. Small twisters appeared like ballet dancers from across the plaza and then, like gleeful children, made for the nearest pile of loose dirt, scattering it into the eyes and ears and shirt fronts of anyone caught to leeward.

But in spite of those minor irritations, working conditions at Zaculeu were excellent. The six-thousand-foot altitude was invigorating to us and to the laborers. Their daily output was far ahead of what could be expected of the same men were they on the hot and humid coast.

We seldom left immediately after quitting time. Instead, we foregathered in one of the small buildings, looked over the day's accomplishments and laid plans for the next day or next week. Often the tourists would wait until evening to visit the ruins, the convenient (for them) moment to catch us when we could not refuse to spend time with them. Manuel, our guardian, had his coterie of locals to chaperone. He revelled in his concoctions of mysteries concerning the ruins. Truth was not beguiling and was more difficult to remember or repeat.

Daniel Murcia and Manuel had an amusing contretemps over the methods and manners of raising corn. Manuel owned his little hut on the site and struggled during his off hours with a small garden at his front door. Principal product, of course, was corn. In the meantime, Daniel had married and his family was increasing. He consulted me about asking Manuel to allow him to plant a few rows of corn in his patch. Manuel was agreeable. Daniel brought out his own seed and prepared the ground for three rows of corn. He brought rich earth from a spot near the river. Manuel had planted his seed in the same rocky soil and in the same manner for years.

Shortly thereafter, Daniel's corn broke the surface in bright green healthy leaves, and was a foot high before Manuel's appeared. In a few weeks Daniel had stalks seven feet high with promising big ears, while Manuel's offered the usual small ears with runty cobs no longer than a man's finger. One morning I asked Manuel how he accounted for Daniel's corn as compared with his. Without hesitation he replied, "Senor Dimick — Manuel is a foreman. He is a foreman who has more time than I who am a laborer. With Daniel's spare time he can say many more Hail Marys than I who must work." That ended the matter.

Our little home in Huehuetenango was beginning to take shape, and Trik and I were ready to leave the hotel and move into our casita. The walls had been scrubbed down and repainted in the usual sort of Pompeian red and sky blues. The little patio and its garden had been beautified by cutting the grass and weeds and pruning the plantain tree. Wild orchids were hanging by wire from the patio roof; their well-laden wire baskets, affording air and moisture as in the wild, had thick moss linings.

We now had an inviting and cozy spot to come home to in the evenings instead of the single rooms at the hotel. A weekend trip to the market in Momostenango produced colorful Indian blankets for beds and floors. We loaded one bed with small pillows over the blanket and hauled it into our tiny sitting room where it doubled for a sofa. In the city we found cane bottoms for chairs and had our carpenter make the frames. We adorned the shelf around our small chimney in the corner with the best of our stone and pottery discoveries. If a decorator in New York wished to duplicate in value what we displayed on that fireplace he would resort to the rarest Dresden or Crown Derby (if comparative costs were a factor).

We found an eight-cubic-foot kerosene refrigerator in Guatemala and on the days when it condescended to work it produced a mushy substance which could just be called ice.

Trik rigged our bathroom in an ingenious fashion. He built a platform in the small kitchen patio, next to our water well. He installed two fifty-gallon tanks on it and ran a small pipe from the tanks down to our large wood-burning cooking stove. There he put a coil of the pipe, making a number of turns, in the fire box where it would be covered by the flame and hot ashes. The pipe continued from the stove through the wall and into the shower head of the bathroom. Our yard boy kept the tanks full in peril of his skin, and when we returned hot and dusty in the evening the cook would have a roaring fire going and the red hot coil provided us with blistering water. Our narrow dining room had room for only six chairs. When eight were needed, we borrowed from the lounge, a not too infrequent occasion.

Edith Baker, our loyal secretary, had her own nest across the patio, from where she took over the housekeeping chores. She treated us like her sons, our spontaneous bad behavior affording her the occasional giggles and blushes which made us love her. On weekends when there was little to do but search a bit deeper into our bottles for relaxation (a privilege we scrupulously refrained from during the week) Trik would produce a succulent martini with dry sherry and the top quality English gin which we were able to get in the city. Trik with his dry manner and enforced frown would gaze at Miss Baker — "Miss Baker," he would drawl, "this must be my last martini; you're beginning to look far too desirable." It seemed almost unethical to drink in Guatemala in those days when the best gin was twenty-five dollars a case and excellent Scotch only thirty; a paradise, however, soon to be lost under the succeeding political regime.

By careful screening of our visitors during the day at the ruins, we supplied ourselves with the promising ones to bring home. We had few regrets, except an occasional squeamish pair who doubted the bug-proofness of our water. An inquiry of that nature categorized the prospect and we didn't take the trouble to explain that our water was carefully filtered. There were just too many venturesome ones anxious to come in preference to their dingy hotel.

We agreed on a house law: no talk of shop was allowed during cocktails or dinner. Nathalie and Dick Woodbury were ensconced in their little house close-by, and they had breakfast and dinner with us. Both were excellent conversationalists and, since we had only occasional newspapers and almost no radio news, our conversations brought out some stimulating philosophies and reminiscences and many arguments.

Father Allié of the local Catholic church and his faithful and hard-working Brother Felix were frequent guests for dinner. Father Allié, a Maryknoller, had been imprisoned in Japan during the war. He was never at a loss for a good yarn, especially under the stimulus of two of Aubrey's martinis. We also dined in his quarters. After one dinner, he took me aside and explained a predicament with which he hoped we could help. He had been to the ruins and seen us making our concrete blocks. If he could only get a few of those, he could build an altar in the small chapel, so badly needed when the big church was not available or the function was not sufficiently important to open it. Could we possibly let him buy some of the blocks?

Father Allié was not so innocent that he thought we could sell blocks or any other supply or equipment from the job. Neither did he think that we would let him down entirely. He was therefore completely satisfied with my promise to think the problem over and let him know. A few days later I told him he could expect the blocks and asked which day would be convenient. Saturday would be best for us, when the truck would not be needed and the men, for a bit of overtime, would help load and unload, or possibly some of his parishioners who worked at the ruins would donate a bit of time. The following Saturday was agreed upon.

We loaded the truck not only with the blocks, but also with bags of white cement and all the necessary tools for the masonry. Two of our best masons went along. During the weekend our men completed the entire altar. Catholic priests, like all heads of church, are accustomed to donations of one kind or another, but that fine man, secluded in a small town and with a minimum of funds, was overwhelmed by this simple and, for us, inexpensive gesture. He displayed his enviable sense of humor when he said in thanks, "It is too bad you are not of my faith; we could name this altar the altar of St. Dimick."

The archaeologist in Central America, and particularly where the Maya ruins are involved, requires two skills. The first, of course, is the ability to observe and properly record his finds, to fit them into what is already known from previous research by himself or others and to recognize his discoveries and their portent as new and as an enlargement of the existing record. His second essential skill is the capability for meticulous search for building phases and changes, and the measurement of those phases, for final drawing and mapping. The combination of these two is often found in one man when that man has the time for the study and recording necessary to both. But the ideal complement is two men, each devoted to his specialty.

At Zaculeu, we had such a combination in Trik and Woodbury. Both knew enough about the other's field to be of enormous mutual help and each was a highly proficient man in his own area. Aubrey Trik's recording of a small temple on the east side of the ruins, and Woodbury's subsequent classification of the pottery recovered by Trik from the multiple aspects of that temple were a classic example of expert teamwork.

This little temple, which we hoped to restore in its last phase, was nothing but a grass-covered mound when we attacked it. Our exploratory trench into the mound at ground level first came upon a small, solid, block-like affair not much larger than a card table. That tiny flat block was the first of twelve superimposed buildings of various shapes and increasing sizes up to the final platform floor at the top, which supported a temple. I watched with increasing admiration while Trik defined that first bit of Maya construction and, as the trench enlarged in height and width, he carefully troweled and brushed his way to added stairways and walls, vertical and horizontal accretions. There were cases where only an added floor constituted a chronological change of fifty years or more. The original boxlike platform ballooned by stages into larger and larger buildings. Each new structure contained either pots or potsherds which gave Woodbury his clues to the ages of or the disparity of years between the twelve buildings.

One field of research was a check upon the other, not a guarantee of exact ages but the most dependable method at Zaculeu, since no modern dating methods were available to us then.

As our research neared the top of the building and the temple which had been there, we uncovered our first cremation burials. How the Indians cremated their dead is not certain. Probably they simply burned the body in a hot wood fire and recovered the skeletal remains afterward. Cremation burials, however, were fairly standard at our operation. The bones were charred beyond recognition, then broken into small fragments. They were stuffed into an urn somewhat the size of a gallon jar. A hole was cut into the floor of the selected burial site. The urn was placed in the hole and the floor was crudely patched with plaster. Different from our modern burials of the kind was the ritual of placing gifts in the urn. The cremation burials in this temple contained stone beads, small copper bells, bone needles, and in one urn a small copper plaque. Small carved jades appeared frequently. But the urn which produced the gold butterfly was the most exciting of all. Dr. Kidder was there that day when we found and removed the plaster patch. We asked him to lift and empty the urn. As the charred bones poured forth, the butterfly, still shining after 800 years, fell in Dr. Kidder's hand. He was nonplussed for a moment. Then looking up at us standing over him he said, "Boys, in twenty-five years of digging, this is the first gold I have personally uncovered."

When we were satisfied that there were no more urn burials beneath the final floor we faced the restoration of the temple. During the examination of the trench we had at the same time cleaned the outer sides of the platform and found ample evidence to rebuild the terraces and stairs. But the discovery of the temple facade was theatrical. Trik had been carefully scratching about at the top, obviously frustrated, for several days. What had happened up there? Were we faced with the unhappy prospect of simply clearing away the debris and leaving a flat-topped affair with little or no character? Dramatically the answer came. The entire front of the temple had been laid down gently almost in one piece on the top of the platform, by a merciful earthquake! It had folded forward like a closing box lid. There it lay from bottom to top. We had the answer and everything began to confirm the theory. Measurements fitted as expected. There was no debris between the floor and that thick layer of stone and mortar, which further proved that it must have fallen quickly. It was no problem to pick up the front wall, stone by stone, and restore it to its original position. Large chunks of white plaster proved again that this temple, like the others, was a proud example of meticulous research and rebuilding.

Our treasures were accumulating in the office at an alarming rate. If we should have a fire or an earthquake, or possibly a robbery, the National Museum in Guatemala would hold us accountable. We approached the officials there for direction on what to do with our increasing hoard. After some weeks of indecision on the part of the National Museum, we decided to build our own museum at the site.

We constructed a small but strong building of adobe with well timbered roof members covered with the native red tile. The walls were plastered a Zaculeu white, a concrete floor was laid and the windows heavily screened. Plate glass showcases were obtained and placed on locally built cabinets with doors and padlocks. In the cases we displayed groupings of the best preserved and most unusual pieces. In one corner we reassembled one of our urn burials. We cut the huge urn vertically in half and displayed the sitting skeleton within, surrounded by all the gifts which had been interred with him originally. We displayed our best incense burners on individual pedestals. One case contained a life-size section of the great tomb with every piece placed exactly as it was found. Woodbury put together a collection of what he called trade pieces, pottery and artifacts which had been brought to Zaculeu from remote cities from the sixth to the ninth century. Trik drew a colored map on the bottom of the glass case with Zaculeu as its hub. The selected pieces were then placed on the map at the points where we considered them to have originated. I believe that such an expedient is good practice for any archaeological museum, regardless of size. Each exhibit was labeled in simple, straightforward fashion in Spanish and English. We put a guest book on a table in the Museum. By the time we had completed our field work we had 3,124 signatures in the book, which I am sure represented no more than a third of the people who had visited the museum by that time, a minute fraction of the numbers since.

Only once during our almost three years of activity at Zaculeu did we run afoul of the bared teeth of political enmity towards our own country by the Guatemalan government as it was then constituted. It came as a disturbing shock to us at Zaculeu. The United Fruit Company office in Guatemala called me by phone to say that the morning paper carried headlines on the front page charging that the Americans were ruining the site at Zaculeu and were painting the buildings white. Typical of sensational papers, the bold type provides the scare headlines which the text is seldom able to maintain. However, the dirt was done and the United Fruit Company was justifiably outraged. I went to Guatemala at once to confer with William Taillon, general manager of the Company for Central America, a man who had been our sincere ally and staunch friend throughout.

Mr. Taillon was all for announcing that the work would be suspended until the source of this erroneous and unfair allegation could be determined.

Fortunately the editor of the paper was amiable; he could and was willing to give us the source which, of course, turned out to be persons with no responsibility, political cronies of the extreme leftist president.

Our approach and defense had to be, of necessity, delicate. We first went to the museum where the director, a recognized archaeologist, and his assistant had offices. They had seen the article and were not surprised to see us. I insisted that we all take the first airplane to Zaculeu for full inspection of the work. We had been working almost two years and neither of these men had even paid a courtesy call to the ruins. They reluctantly agreed to come. We took them, a representative from the United Fruit Company, and two members of the press, with photographers. We spent a full day at the ruins, explaining in detail the research which had guided us to the type of restoration we were doing. Fortunately, we had carefully preserved areas on each building where the white mortar placed there by the Maya was in full evidence. The reporters and photographers were having a field day. They realized that this was a crisis and that they had best have all the information in case the conflict should, as they secretly hoped, get out of hand.

Those in power were soon convinced, reluctantly perhaps, that our work was properly done and in good archaeological taste. "It is a shame that such an indictment has gotten to the press and public." This off-the-cuff apology was not enough for Taillon and me; we insisted on a public retraction, and in the same paper. This was agreed to and the retraction was made but, as we expected, it consisted of one column, three inches on an inside page. No headlines for the defendant.

Midway of the second season at Zaculeu two visitors appeared. The men were unknown to each other except for their publications, but quickly became friends and provided reciprocal assistance in their research. The first was Dr. Charles Goff from Hartford, Connecticut, a recognized expert in orthopedic research and surgery. The second was Dr. T. Dale Stewart, head of the division of physical anthropology at the Smithsonian Institution.

Our association with Dr. Goff, which led to his invaluable contribution to our final report, was accidental. He and Mrs. Goff were on a winter tour of Central America. Dr. Goff had heard of the work in progress at Zaculeu and, being an archaeological enthusiast, he departed from the usual tours set up by the agencies in order to visit us.

After politely examining the digging, he shyly let us know that his real interest lay in our skeletal material, that he was a practicing orthopedic surgeon. I told him that if he would rearrange his schedule and spend the night in Huehuetenango, we would be pleased to have him examine our bone collection which we considered well catalogued and indexed. When we told him that there were thirty or more classified skeletons already on hand, he needed no further persuasion.

Here again was an example of the reward for carefully registering and preserving bone groups and for the dating of them by their association with artifacts of established epoch.

We left Charles Goff in the office that day and when we returned, he was ecstatic. Could he please stay another few days? He did, until his vacation time was exhausted and he had passed up numbers of other points of interest which had been on his itinerary, in order to turn his vacation into a vocational exercise. When he left he asked if he might return the following season, and I was enthusiastic over the prospect.

We felt that, if invited, Charles would contribute to our final publication, but none of us dreamed how sensational one part of his contribution would be. After a few weeks' study the following year, and after his examination of additional skeletons which had been unearthed since his last visit, he made his announcement one evening at our house. He was prepared to state that syphilis existed at Zaculeu hundreds of years before Columbus! It had *not* been introduced by the Spaniards. His expert knowledge of bone deformations caused by the disease in modern man convinced him that what he found here must come from the same malady. When we recovered from the news Charles told us that there had been other diagnoses of similar character in the western hemisphere, but that the theory had been handled gingerly because of the uncertainty of the dates of the disinterred skeletons. Here at Zaculeu we had provided him with the positive dating he needed.

Charles wrote two articles for our final publication: one, highly technical, a study of the entire skeletal complex at Zaculeu. The other was his explosive exposé of the syphilitic findings. He explains in his article all of the methods used in testing for the disease, and finishes his thesis by stating that two cranial specimens were found in the ruins of Zaculeu which show gross evidence of destructive lesions compatible with the diagnosis of bone syphilis. He goes on to say in his summary, in the simple fashion which we all prefer hearing from our doctors, "Historical evidence points towards the western hemisphere as the origin of syphilis as against a European origin."

Dr. T. Dale Stewart, head of the National Museum's department of anthropology at the Smithsonian, made two visits to Zaculeu. The keen interest which this learned man displayed in our skeletal inventory is best emphasized by the fact that, after his visit in 1947 when he could devote only six days to his investigations, he returned in 1948 for a much longer stay. Dr. Stewart displayed additional proof of his high evaluation of our material when his meticulously taken photographs were spoiled during development and he returned to repeat laboriously that painstaking work.

With his enviable knowledge and his careful research, he gave us the number of individuals, even their ages and sex in instances where, as often was the case, our graves were a jumbled mass of broken bones. Some graves had been re-used as much as fifty years later without being depleted of the remains of the earlier tenants. Our regular crew included no such expert. Until Dr. Stewart arrived and made his analysis we had saved everything for fear of discarding some valuable specimens unrecognized by our staff. At our request, Dr. Stewart separated the valuable from the worthless and handed us piles of bones which could be discarded with assurance. They were reinterred at the site. Dr. Stewart discovered numerous patterns of dental mutilation performed by the aborigines and prepared the drawings for publication. In the afternoons at the office or on weekends when we were supposed to be busy with our own note-keeping or mapping, it was difficult to restrain ourselves from peering over the shoulder of Dr. Stewart at his work of reassembling the skeletal framework from what appeared to us an unfathomable mass. But nothing demonstrated his anatomical skills as graphically as did his handling of the crushed and burned skulls which were found in the cremation jars. The double handful of bits of skull fragments, few of which were larger than a man's thumb nail, under his magic handling would begin to take shape, each tiny piece carefully glued to its neighbor until almost the entire skull evolved. Not only was Doctor Stewart able to put this grisly jigsaw puzzle together, but when he had finished the work was so perfect he could distinguish deformities which had existed on the living head.

Without contributions such as those made by Doctors Goff and Stewart, the final report on Zaculeu would have been distressingly incomplete.

The curtain was about to descend on Zaculeu. We could have continued to dig and restore for years, but it was agreed that incidence of repetition was to be expected and the additional time and effort would be comparatively unrewarding. We had examined and partially restored at least one of each of the various types of buildings encountered and the whole ruin had taken on the appearance which had been our objective, — to leave it as a ruin with a significant degree of restoration to afford tourists and visitors an idea of its original appearance.

At the end of my introduction to our published report on Zaculeu, which appeared in 1953, I wrote these words which were more prophetic than I knew: "Since the fall of Zaculeu in the sixteenth century, other empires have decayed or suddenly fallen, crowns have tottered and entire global concepts have been altered. Those powerful Indian dynasties, once secure and aloof from political ideologies, collapsed under the might of organized warfare, impelled by a fanatical religious impulse. Nothing but peonage remained. Down through the succeeding centuries we have witnessed similar intrusions instigated and inspired by changing political theory, and accomplished by force."

I then quoted Doris Stone who made the dedicatory address at Zaculeu in 1948 when we handed the ruins over to the Guatemalan Government as a National Park. Doris, you will remember, is the daughter of Samuel Zemurray.

"To begin with, we must call attention to the fact that these ruins represent what in one period was a prosperous center of trade and religion. In truth, at the beginning, it was the first factor, trade, that originated the foundation of such cities. It is this branch of human endeavor that has been responsible for the most outstanding events in the development of the entire world.

"Here, years before the Christian era, the Inca, the Maya and the Aztec trafficked in foodstuff and materials and opened long roads of commerce which gave free entry and enforced times of peace even among nations torn by internecine wars."

Dr. Kidder came to the ruins during the last days at Zaculeu. One morning he was sitting in the shade of a small building, writing in his little black book, the diary for which he was so famous. (Those diaries, unfortunately, have never been published.) When Ted was writing in his little black book it was a signal never to interrupt. But on that morning when I was walking by at a discreet distance he called me over and asked me to sit down. "John," he asked, "have you been to Tikal?" My answer was "No." "You must go," said Ted. "Tikal is the greatest of all the Mayan cities and it should be restored. John, I don't know anyone but you to undertake the organization and financing of such a colossal project. I hope you will think about it."

Those words of Ted Kidder were to be realized seven years later when the curtain would rise on another drama in Guatemala with a bit part reserved and waiting for me. But what I had forecast with impatience as a long period between shows was not to to be. There came a call from Philadelphia—

Memphis

RUDOLPH ANTHES, German scholar and Professor of Egyptology at the University of Pennsylvania, would soon retire. His success with the University as a teacher had been limited. He was in full command of his subject, but probably because of his rather ponderous accent he had difficulty maintaining class interest and imparting to his lectures enough of entertainment quality to hold his dwindling attendance. His pupils, at one point, were down to two.

Pressure was on Froelich Rainey, University Museum Director. The post called for a younger man, who could attract and maintain student interest. What to do? Retire Anthes forthwith? No, that is not Rainey's way. He resists to the last any decision that may hurt or embarrass. Would Anthes lead an archaeological expedition to Egypt? Of course he would. His Arabic was adequate though heavily steeped, as was his English, in his native tongue. But his many Egyptian friends and fellow scholars spoke German. In fact some of them had studied with him in Germany before the war. He would head a dig in Egypt. Retirement age was near, and Rainey would be searching for a replacement and Anthes' dignity would be unimpaired. Happy solution for all.

Rainey asked me to come to Philadelphia. He knew of our management system at Zaculeu. Would I become Director of the Museum's dig to start soon in Egypt?! Anthes could direct the field work; Henry Fisher as assistant was already an expert at classifying and correlating the finds. (Henry's skill has since been adjudged and rewarded by his being made Curator of Egyptian Art at the Metropolitan Museum.) Jean Jaquet, French architect, was available for tomb and structural recordings. But management and its kindred details were of no interest to Anthes. That was my job. With my usual recklessness I accepted.

The Museum owned a large house in the Nile valley at Mit Rahineh. It had been headquarters many years before when Sir Flinders Petrie was excavating there. It could be refurbished and lived in. The dig would be nearby. My wife Teena and I heard all this from across Rainey's desk in the summer of 1954. That fall we were on our way to Cairo via Japan and Thailand, certainly the two most ill-coached bit players ever to step onto a stage where such dramatic personages as Rameses, Moses and Cleopatra among others had composed the original cast.

When we arrived in Cairo, Anthes had already selected his site for digging at Memphis, ancient capital of Egypt. The house was only a quarter mile away. We met in Cairo and agreed on how I could best serve him and the project. The house had to be refurbished, equipment located and purchased within our skimpy budget, and regular transportation established between the dig and Cairo. Our funds would be deposited in the city twenty-five miles away and dealt out locally for payrolls.

There was no hardship involved in this arrangement for the Dimicks. We set up headquarters in an apartment at the old

Semiramis Hotel, top floor, overlooking the Nile, the Pyramids in the distance, unusual fare for supposed desert archaeologists. Part of our living room was converted into my office with desk and drawing table. Anthes had asked that part of my participation include mapping of the Memphis area around the site.

We were in most august company on our floor. All of it except our tiny portion was living quarters for King Saud of Saudi Arabia. We shied around his dark-skinned guards who stared suspiciously at us from their sentry positions at every door between the elevator and our own entrance. We never understood and were not told why the king failed to absorb our two rooms along with the thirty or more he commanded on the floor.

By the weekend we were unpacked and Monday I was on the town with Anthes, helping purchase final items for the house: canned food, meager electric wire and 25-watt bulbs, tinny knives and forks, a small refrigerator and other fare which the Cairo market provided. During that week we commuted to Memphis by taxi, experiencing the usual mishaps, flat tires, over-heated engines, empty gas tanks and whatever can happen to old automobiles suffering from constant abuse and lack of parts. Next week Teena provided the big lift when she purchased for ourselves and for the project a new Opel station wagon. From then on we skimmed over the desert roads, wind- and sandproofed, the envy of all. We could move at will.

The hotel gamely attempted box lunches. Teena rounded them out by robbing our breakfast trays of morsels systematically over-ordered. After the city chores were done and items on Anthes' list from the day before collected, we rolled up the Nile in dust-proof luxury to the dig.

Our picnic lunches were true situation comedies. Any place near the road was unbearable. The slightest disturbance, even a running barefoot child, set off a cloud of rising dry silt of unbearable density. The Arab farmers, the fellahin, owned the scattered coconut palms and lived among or near them. We would leave the road at noon and settle under a palm where its sparse and lofty foliage, forty feet above us, projected a round dot of shade about the size of our station wagon. Then, during lunch and the cigarette afterwards, we would move the car a few feet at a time, maintaining our position clockwise in the moving shadow a hundred and eighty degrees off the sun. The local children and dogs quickly learned our midday habits and were on hand for their share. We could not refuse or discourage them, but the prideful parents of the children would not condone their begging and sternly called them away.

An American oil company office in Cairo lent me a transit, level rod and tape for my survey. After a few days of lingering hungrily over the huge pit being dug by Anthes and company, and marveling at the antlike line of black men in their white cotton galabeas, carrying out the dirt in their small baskets, I realized there was no part here for me. I could serve best by being a silent director, leaving these men to their skills. I had my bilingual native helper and proceeded with my survey.

My traverse went along well. Soon a pattern developed, a huge walled rectangle, the walls of adobe blocks. It extended some three miles north and south by a half mile east and west. It could be defined now only by the sporadic showing of some badly eroded sections.

After the recognizable segments had been surveyed and plotted there seemed no question that the wall had been complete in early times. How to be sure? We had met at some social function a Captain in the Egyptian Air Force. He had been interested in our job or had at least expressed interest while talking with Teena. If he would only fly over some day and take a picture of the area. Nothing could be lost in asking. With my map in hand, I called on him at his barracks. "Captain," I said, "during the last war our air force photographed every foot of the Nile valley. If I were in Washington, I am sure I could get a picture of this section. But even in America it would require weeks, and yards of red tape. Since the section is not critical, do you suppose you could either let me see a picture from the Egyptian files or, better still, could you have one taken for me?"

He smiled at my long winded approach. "Mr. Dimick, if you were oriental you could not have taken longer to get to the point. I'll take it myself."

"Captain, if you would do that, what about doing it in mid-morning? I want the shadows to the west in order to bring out the wall." Two days later my phone rang from the lobby. The Captain was there with a blown up photograph of the site. Over a coffee we compared the picture with the survey and there, clear and certain, were the missing wall sections. Without the photograph they could have been dotted in on the map, a symbol of conjecture, but now they were a certainty. Gaps in the shadows could well have been gates. I could now draw the entire enclosure, but what was it?

"You have the confines of the wall of the Temple of Ptah," announced Anthes when he saw the map. "And our present digging, according to your plot, should soon disclose the outside southwest corner." He was right and within a few days the enormous wall appeared and took shape. It was a monstrous affair, some thirty feet wide at its base. When built it must have been eighteen to twenty feet high and battered to a crown width of ten to eleven feet, all of well formed baked adobe blocks. Now the remains of the ruined buildings within the wall must be mapped. Fortunately, for the benefit of the whole survey, I started at the north and worked south. A fine palace of King Apries had stood at the north end in the days of his reign, 588 to 568 B.C. Nothing remained but its heavy adobe walls, now badly quarried by the farmers who find the adobe rich in fertilizing agents. On or near the top were sections of enormous limestone columns with lotus leaf capitals, mute evidence of the grandeur that once was. Other buildings could be located but only sketched in because of poor evidence. One beautiful entrance building was completely flattened, with its finely carved columns and lintels floundering now in a lake of Nile seepage. The base of a perfectly preserved statue of Rameses could be mapped; the statue had been carefully removed and now rests in the plaza at the Cairo railway station.

Then, at the south end of the temple, I found my building, the one to become my own private enterprise. If I had found it earlier it would have been difficult to neglect it for so mundane an effort as a simple survey. There near the southwest corner of the temple wall lay the partially uncovered floor and a few scatttered standing features of the Embalming House of the Apis Bulls!

Having no idea what it was, that afternoon I asked Anthes and Fisher about it. They told me its name. Neither showed the slightest interest in the building except to say that practically nothing had been written about it. They did suggest some primer type reading for me on Apis Bulls and their part in history. No doubt they agreed (and rightly) that, with my survey finished, this new interest would occupy me nicely. Structural research just does not hold the interest for researchers that do the tools and everyday accoutrement of the ancient inhabitants. A pity sometimes. But my spirits were soon to receive a substantial boost. The scholars were digging away with limited success around the wall corner. A small burial appeared here and there with its correspondingly light ornamentation, some simple house rooms with their floors yielding domestic pottery. All the time the digging was being hampered, even held up as it went deeper, by the encroachment of the Nile.

At this point Percy Madeira, Chairman of the Board of Managers of the Museum, and his wife Eugenia arrived from Philadelphia. Percy was a working Chairman. He went into the field to appraise a job in his own fashion. He never presented himself as an expert, but he knew what was good for the Museum, and when appropriated funds were producing adequate dividends.

The dig at Mit Rahineh. Remains of the great wall are visible in center of photograph.

Above: Porters carry dirt to waiting dump cart as passing villagers look on.

Left: Egyptology has developed an expert few who are specialists in skillful excavating. Many of them, such as the one shown here, are from the town of Guft and are respectfully called "Guftis." No properly conducted dig is without its "Gufti."

Opposite Page: The dig at Mit Rahineh. Shadowed diagonal through center is remains of the west wall of Temple of Ptah near its S.W. corner.

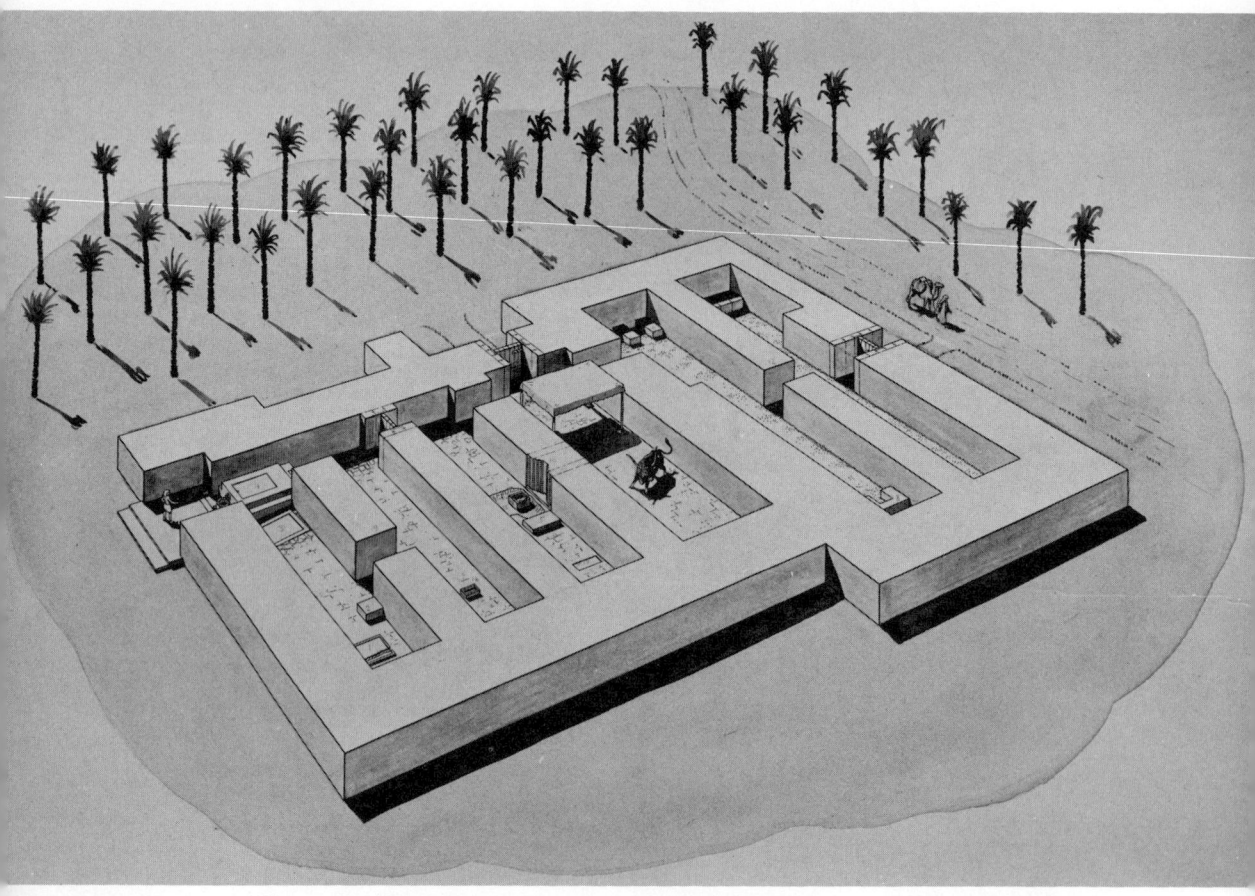

Above: The Embalming House remains show no signs of having been roofed. From the floor plans and highest standing wall the drawing illustrates how the palace and embalming areas were combined.

Top Right: N.E. corner of Embalming House. The deceased bull was probably carted through the gate to the waiting embalming table in the corner.

Bottom right: A late embalming table of alabaster. These blocks weighed over fifty tons. Note the drain spout and alabaster receptacle used for collecting the bull's blood; also the high relief lion which runs the full length of the table. In the foreground is a used and discarded table. Neither table has been dated.

GIZA

Left: The lifting gear can be seen resting on its track as chain is lowered toward carefully cleaned stones.

Above: Shed erected over the lifting gear. Pyramid of Cheops is at right of picture.

Right: Gear is tested as a stone is lifted for the first time.

Above left: Professor Abubakr carefully brushes a stone in search of identifying marks.

Above right: The author watches as a hoist is rigged.

Opposite Page: Chain hoists hang from trolley as workmen guide them into position over stones.

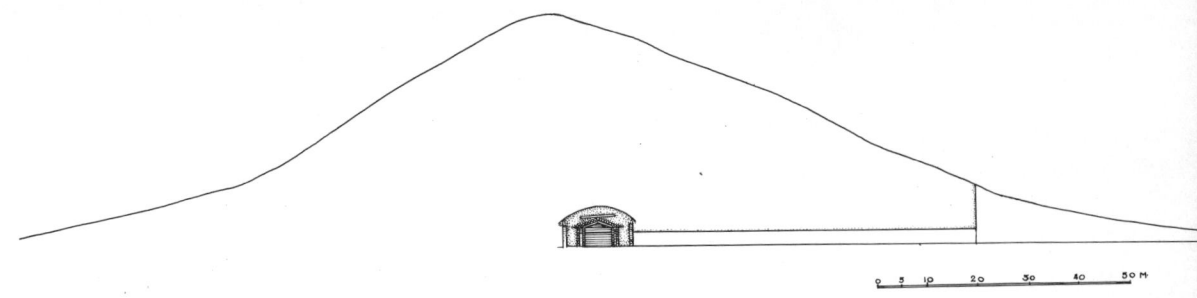

A three-foot stone wall stood apart and the space between was filled with pebbles and rubble.

In this richly furnished tomb the king lay on a wooden bier. His body had been wrapped in a vestment, now disintegrated. A faint odor of cedar was still present around the collapsed and decayed bier.

Left: Profile of the great earthen mound at Gordion. Top: drawing shows location of tomb and combination trench and tunnel dug to reach it. The mound is 155 feet high and 891 feet in diameter.

TARQUINIA

Left: Electric drill bores through overburden to puncture roof of a tomb.

Bottom Left: The periscope is lowered through auger hole into tomb. If the periscope survey discloses anything worth recording, a Minox camera is lowered on the same shaft and a panorama photograph taken.

Bottom right: An archaeologist peers through the periscope. He moves in a complete circle to examine the tomb's periphery.

Opposite Page: This picture, showing one corner of a tomb, was taken through a bore hole with the Minox attached to the persicope shaft. The debris in the foreground is from the collapsed roof of the tomb.

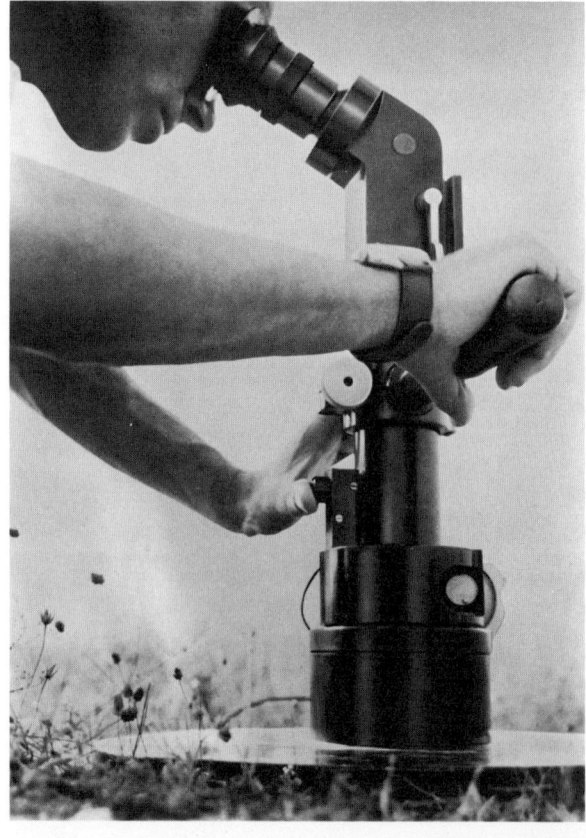

Above: Aubrey Trik at work with the proton magnetometer.

Opposite Page: The quad system for digging was best on the gentle Kythera slopes.

KYTHERA *In the afternoon Huxley, right, and crew examine potsherds from the day's diggings. Indicative ones are catalogued immediately—the rest discarded.*

Memphis

The Madeiras put up at the Semiramis. Percy lingered long over my map which was now finished, and the next day we took them to the dig.

Percy leaned over to look into the crater-like excavation with its now constantly muddy floor. "What do you have?" he asked.

"The southwest corner of the Temple of Ptah," came the answer.

"What else?"

"That's about all at the moment," came the hesitant reply. What else does one say to the Chairman of the Board?

After a moment Percy turned away and with some expletive now forgotten, said to me, "Did we come all the way to Egypt to find the corner of a wall?" We had crossed the road when he queried, "What's this ruin?"

"Percy," I said, "this is my private project allowed me by the boss of excavations. Nobody else had any interest in it. They tell me it is what remains of the Embalming House of the Apis Bulls, whatever that means. I'm going to read up on this sacred fellow and unearth enough of the building to measure it, then write something."

"Well", said Percy, "At least I can *see* this." (The expert digging of Anthes and Fisher continued through two seasons and produced valued additions to the knowledge of ancient Memphis. Later Percy was the first to agree.)

From that morning on I hardly saw the main dig. We carried out our daily logistic assignments, bringing supplies and funds from the city, but now my one passion was this heretofore neglected House. Its skeletal remains, bleaching there in the desert sun, were all that remained of that kind, in Egypt or in the world. There are no duplicates. After a week of digging I had the four corners. From them it was an easy matter to measure and draw in the room walls and standing features. When an ancient Egyptian writing appeared Henry Fisher would come over from the big dig and translate for me.

Bernard Bothmer, now curator of Ancient Art at Brooklyn Museum, then Director of the American Research Center in Cairo, encouraged me and gave valuable suggestions on what may have transpired there within those abstruse walls, based partially upon my findings. It was Bernard for instance who examined four heavy doughnut-like stone circles lying scattered on the floor and surmised that they were used for holding poles which in turn supported a canopy to shade Apis. We had decided earlier that the building had not been roofed and therefore that some sheltering device must have existed to protect the holy bull from the desert sun. I spent a happy month digging and recording that fascinating building. My technical report on it was published in the University Museum's publication on the excavations at Mit Rahineh, modern village over the ruins of ancient Memphis.

But there was more to be reported here than just the study of the house; a chronicle on the Bull himself. *Archaeology Magazine* agreed, and published my story of the living Bull, his caprices, his influence on Egyptian culture and history; a vigorous god who held sway in that bizarre combination of stable, exercise ground and embalming facility where he reigned and, after death, was skilfully prepared for his hereafter. From a coterie of sources I was able to develop a glimpse into the life of Apis. Fact and legend have long been too well homogenized for modern separation.

The God Apis

The Embalming House of the Apis Bulls stood just within the southwest corner of the great wall of Memphis. Today, partially suffocated by the restless silt of the Nile valley, the unique structure rests in comparative obscurity. In its original glory it was a mansion of limestone, probably roofless. It contained embalming tables weighing as much as fifty tons, carved from a single block of alabaster. The structure was dedicated principally to the preservation of the carcass of Apis, sacred bull of Memphis, whose soul was supposed to be the image of the god Osiris. Osiris, whose name means 'Many-eyed,' was one of the important gods of Egyptian mythology. He was Judge of the Dead, Ruler of the Kingdom of Ghosts, God of the Nile and Constant Foe of Evil. He also represented the setting sun.

In olden days the cattle of Egypt were fat, beautiful creatures of varying colors and shades. The rarest were those whose backs and sides were black, with regular stripes of a lighter color on the belly and legs. Such a bull was in high esteem, and it is probable that the bull Apis was so marked. He had a triangular white blaze on his forehead. His horns swept out and upward to perfectly matched points. He was a handsome creature, a blue ribbon winner in any competition. Plutarch thrilled his readers by describing Apis as "born of a ray darting from the moon on his mother who, after his birth, never brought forth again. On his shoulders was the resemblance of an eagle, the mark of a scarab on his tongue and the hairs on his tail were double." No doubt any slight resemblance to any or all of these marking was sufficient to satisfy the credulity of his worshipers.

Although the bull Apis could not live forever, his soul would live on, providing his body was properly preserved. Therefore the creatures of this fabulous animal dynasty were preserved and buried with all the ritualistic fervor given the Pharaohs. In 1851 the famous French Egyptologist, Mariette, discovered their burial place (the Serapeum) high on the desert plateau at Sakkara. Within that enormous excavation are huge sarcophagi carved out of granite or limestone. Each at one time contained the carefully embalmed remains of a deceased Apis. All of these great stone coffins were long ago opened and rifled, but they remain there in their underground resting places, their huge stone lids pushed back, the inscriptions which identify them still legible, telling of the dynasty in which each bull was born, lived and died.

Even before his death, according to Greek historians, Apis' successor had been chosen. Once chosen, the sacred calf was fed on milk for four months, in a house facing the east. At the end of this time, at the new moon, he was transformed to Memphis in a boat bearing a gilded house, amidst the rejoicings of the people. Authorities differ on whether or not the young Apis lived in the same palace with the old one during the last months of his life. We read of a hall being built for Apis, adjoining the temple of Ptah, the chief deity of Memphis. There were two chambers and in front a magnificent court. The bull's food was selected with the greatest care, and lest in his state of confinement he should grow too fat, he was never given "the rich water of the Nile" to drink.

Apis was seldom exposed to the view of curious strangers, only exhibited on solemn festivals when he was led through the city in procession. It was a good omen if he took food readily from those who offered it to him, but evil if he refused it. Public prosperity or calamity was portended by his entering one or the other of his two special apartments. Children vied with each other to have his breath blow upon them and thus receive a gift of prophecy. Those who consulted him for guidance kept their ears closed until they had left the vicinity of the temple, and the first words they heard when they opened them again contained the answer of the god to their inquiry.

Apis' death was a time of general mourning, his interment a costly affair. Superstition reached such heights that the magnificence of the ceremonies proved ruinous to the people. During the reign of the first Ptolemy, for example, all the money appropriated for Apis' funeral was expended, and the people then went heavily in debt to Ptolemy in order to provide additional demonstrations. The Embalming House was a tremendously expensive building, as were its furnishings. It probably contained also the living quarters of Apis and fronted upon an open grazing and exercise area for the bull. The Greek historian Herodotus, writing (ii.153) of his adventures in Egypt in the fifth century B.C., spoke of Psamtik I (663-609 B.C.) who, "having made himself master of all Egypt . . . built a court for Apis, in which he is fed whenever he appears." Herodotus also described the court as surrounded by a colonnade supported by statues instead of pillars, and full of sculptured figures. All this disappeared long ago.

Not until 1941 was a clue found to the actual position of the Embalming House, although fifty years earlier its general location had been surmised. During the lean years of World War II it was understandably difficult to find money for digging. Practically all archaeologists folded their equipment for the duration; they found their excitement in the service of their countries. However, Dr. Ahmad Badawy, one of Egypt's fine historians, did have a small appropriation which he would doubtless have lost had he not used it at once, and he chose to use it for digging in old Memphis. These limited funds were exhausted in less than two months, but in that time he uncovered a sizable part of the floor plan of the Embalming House. Almost a half century before, Sir Flinders Petrie had found the building but his digging was negligible and his report inconclusive. Now my turn had come — no one else in our group seemed to care — "Let Dimick do it."

What could I learn about this badly damaged ruin? Century after century had seen stone robbers depleting walls and furnishings until practically nothing remained. Successive dammings of the Nile and consequent increases in the water level added to the destruction. History was of little help except in providing fascinating legends and mythology. The meager theories concerning the building, its shape and function were based only upon the superficial digging before me. I set out, therefore, to substantiate or to controvert those theories by further digging.

The stone palace where Apis lived, died and was embalmed lay within the walls of the massive Temple of Ptah. Those temple walls were bastions of earth, thirty feet or more at the base and of indeterminate height. Today little remains of them. The southern wall of the Embalming House now touches the winding, dusty road connecting the main north-south highway with the desert. Along this road the Egyptian farmer leads his donkey or camel, just as he did twenty-five hundred years ago when the building was standing. In its entirety, the Embalming House was a rectangle approximately two hundred by one hundred feet, probably not roofed. The exterior walls were lined inside and out with cut limestone blocks, and then filled with either rubble or adobe bricks. The northern, better preserved, half contains most of the remaining evidence; the southern half seems to have been heavily plundered for building stone. Long rooms, separated by thick walls and paved with stones of irregular shapes averaging seven inches in thickness, crossed the building. Heavy stone frames held wooden doors hinged on extensions of their inner edges which fitted into sockets cut into the stone floor. Two rooms containing troughs and manger-like stone vessels were connected by a massive stone door jamb. These may well have been the rooms into which the capricious bull wandered and thus foretold good or evil.

Evidence points to a costly refurnishing program late in the fifth century B.C. Probably the earlier level had been abandoned as the water table rose, and a higher, drier level was imposed upon the earlier one. The great alabaster embalming table in the northeast corner was placed almost exactly where the earlier and less ornate one of limestone had been, except that it was several feet higher. The first table was pushed aside, and it now lies worn, cracked and out of plumb beside its successor. One old embalming table in the northwest corner of the building was crudely cleaved by later stone hunters but its fragments were there, unused.

The one embalming table which had been completed and which also survivied the later foraging for stone is a single block of alabaster, masterfully rendered. Along each side is an elongated lion in high relief. On the top is a shallow recess which gradually deepens towards the end. Here the body fluids were caught and drained off into an alabaster basin. The weight of the block is conservatively estimated at fifty tons. It is another example of the weight-handling genius of the Egyptians, who transported it from the distant quarry near Amarna. Unfortunately, the table bears no inscription. After thousands of years under desert sands no stains or other traces of its actual use remain. However, the older table beside it shows positive signs of having been scraped and cleaned. Two additional tables much like the finished one of alabaster were within the Embalming House but were not adorned, good proof that final sculpturing must have been done after the stones were put in place.

"Apis IS DEAD! Long live the new Apis!" Some such cry no doubt arose upon the announcement of the bull's death. Preparations for the embalming began immediately. The dead Apis was carried from his quarters into an embalming section, let us say in the northeast corner of the building, where he was placed upon the enormous table. We may presume that the head was placed at the south and the four feet upward to expose the body properly for removal of all the organs. Good embalming tactics required that as the first step. Cleaned and ready for mummification, he much resembled the carcass of any fat Angus hanging in the ice box today at your favorite butcher's. The bull's body, like the human, contains about 75 per cent water by weight and, as in the case of the dead Pharaohs, it was necessary first to deplete it of all body fluids, most of which would have drained into the large drum-like alabaster basin at the end of the table. Once cleansed, the carcass was then ready for careful preservation and purification. Most important in the process was the drying. The useful Egyptian sun helped greatly, but it was too slow to be relied upon alone. The absorbent materials easily available in Egypt were lime and salt. No positive proof of the use of lime as an embalming agent has been found, but the use of salt is suggested by good authorities. Certainly some agent was used for an immersion bath, and salt is acceptable. The carcass was then swabbed out with strong salt solution preparatory to packing. Packing was another step in assuring dryness. Such materials as resin, wood pitch or sawdust were packed into the cavities, including the brain cavity. Cotton rags soaked in resin were used for stuffing, and costly spices, such as myrrh and cassia, and aromatic ingredients were placed in the cavity before the final sewing. Then the bull was ready for wrapping. Continuous layers of cloth dipped in liquid resin completed the mummification. How long the embalming required is not known, probably several days. Finally the mummy was placed upon a heavy cart with great wooden wheels, and amid processional splendor was carried high onto the desert plateau to the magnificent Serapeum, burial place of the Apis bulls, where a sarcophagus awaited it. A youthful successor grazed in unmindful peace and prepared to accustom himself to his life of luxury. The date of the bull's birth was recorded exactly, as was that of his death. Occasionally the otherwise uncertain dating of a Pharaoh has been established by reference to the history of Apis and the bull's age when the Pharaoh succeeded to the throne.

Within the walls of the Embalming House a few inscriptions remain which go far to prove its purpose. One inscription shows Anubis, God of the Dead, and a high priest of Ptah named Shed-su-Nefertem, whose name is flanked by cartouches of Sheshonk I (Dynasty XXII). Jackal-headed Anubis (at left) pours a libation from a tall jar, while Shed-su-Nefertem performs a funerary ceremony called "Opening of the Mouth." On either side of this central group is a single row of hieroglyphs which reads: "It was ordered by the great leader of craftsmen, the sem-priest Shed-su-Nefertem, by His Majesty to cause to be built a wabet-house (purification hall) for his father, the Osiris-Apis, as an excellent work." On another face of the same group of stones are two cartouches of Rameses II (Dynasty XIX), and to the left of those names is a worn inscription in which the name of Apis can be read.

On the remains of an alabaster block in the northwest corner of the Embalming House an inscription proclaims that Amasis (568-525 B.C.) prepared for "his father, the living Apis" a block of alabaster of Hatnub (the well known alabaster quarry near Amarna). Above are the names of articles used in the funerary ritual and the embalming. The fact that Apis was embalmed is best established by some of the Apis stelae found in the vault of the Serapeum. "The sacred corpse was embalmed with spices and the cere-cloths were of byssus, the fabric most becoming for all the gods." There are numerous references to the elaborate burial ceremonies and to the costly sarcophagi. One stela says in part: ". . . Under the reign of Amasis, who bestows life forever, the god Apis was carried in peace to the good region of the west. His interment in the netherworld was accomplished in the place which His Majesty had prepared. Never had the like been done since early times, after they had fulfilled for him all that is customary in the halls of purification."

Apis was worshipped with fluctuating fanaticism from the Second Dynasty until well into the Ptolemaic period—more than two thousand years. It is frustrating that no other building in all the land can be identified as having served the same purpose as this one. The long period during which Apis was worshipped greatly overlaps the estimated period when his embalming occurred. Judging from the earliest date we have, we can say only that the practice of embalming Apis bulls had begun during Dynasty XIX, more precisely about 1300 B.C. The latest mention of Apis which could imply his "purification" dates from the reign of Nectanebo in Dynasty XXX, about 370 B.C. There is some speculation that the ritual may have continued into the early Ptolemaic period. In any case a thousand years is a moderate conjecture. It is unfortunate that more data cannot be recovered having to do with the Embalming House and Serapeum, since they were so clearly associated. One strong argument for their relationship is that Rameses II, whose cartouche is found in the Embalming House, constantly strove to promote the worship of Apis, and his constructions did include the Serapeum. Countless questions concerning the adventures of Apis and his life and death are still unanswered, but the combination of fact and surmise provides a plausible account. What actually took place may remain forever buried along with other mysteries of the desert.

In early December, conveniently near Christmas, I contracted a severe hernia. We returned to New York for the operation and the incidental holiday visit with the family. In early January we were back in Cairo. To that point we had neglected the other Egypt. Now there was little for me to do at Memphis. My part had already been much more exciting than I had any reason to expect when that strange directorship was undertaken. It was time to show Teena the Nile's wonders.

We went up the river by train to Assuan, Karnak and Luxor. One afternoon we wandered into a small shop, selling everything from bad reproductions to good cotton weavings. In a dingy corner were some well-thumbed volumes on Egyptian history by various authors and dated before the turn of the century in most cases. Skimming through one of them aimlessly, I saw the word "Memphis." The books were so surprisingly inexpensive we bought all of them, seven or eight. Each had some references to Memphis, none long or complete. "Dear," I suggested, "you could and should write a story about Memphis. There is no definitive history of that first Capitol of Egypt." Teena demurred and I persisted. "Everyone praises your letter-style and your fine way of expressing yourself; please do. We'll collect all the books we can here, more when we get back home and, after all, who has spent more time there than you?" She agreed to try.

The result was published a year later and fully lived up to her capabilties, brilliant, clear writing following an educated sense of research. Unfortunately, the book was mangled by miserable editing, but even that could not detract from Teena's beautiful English and phraseology.

We returned home in late spring of 1955 feeling like veterans but realizing how far removed we were from being Egyptologists and what it requires in devoted study and years of preparation to be one. Like a ballet dancer, one must start at youth, but even with a life of study there must be that certain ingredient, a basic aptitude for it. Of all the scholars and students of ancient man, the accomplished Egyptologist seems to be the rarest.

Some writing of mine in the remote past contained a phrase about science in general hurdling international boundaries. To my best knowledge, it was original. If not, its source escapes me. The scientists' subscription to that belief, which would be rated political heresy, has been faithfully demonstrated in Egypt. The sciences circumvent political frontiers when they don't choose to ignore them, which is more often. Our two seasons in Egypt were ones of delightful camaraderie with our Arab counterparts. Our mutual goal was the enlightenment of man, our aim to assist each other, sharing and exchanging information. There was no subterfuge, no double talk. Proper Museum people, be they from their chemical or physics laboratories, their geophysical research or on down the scale to simple archaeology, if unrestricted by politics will lecture on or write what they believe, withholding no knowledge or conclusions. Progress is made of such stuff.

When Secretary Dulles, brimming with misinformation, uttered his calamitous dictum, "An agonizing reappraisal," and thus irretrievably squandered America's hope for Egyptian friendship, there was not a ripple in scholastic circles there. Today when our governmental relationship with Cairo has reached the dregs of deterioration, the cultural groups here are struggling to provide America's share of hard dollars for preservation of Abu Simbel. The United States drops some of its counterpart funds into the pot because we have nothing else to do with our prodigious balance of Egyptian pounds, which must be spent in Egypt only.

Our science is pleased with its happy friendship with the Egyptian scholars and their Department of Antiquities. The University of Pennsylvania Museum has lived with, negotiated with and collaborated with them for close to forty years with no more serious argument than how much track or how many dump carts they were to supply, or equally trivial matters, settled amicably on the spot.

The fact that we work there, aloof from the manufactured hatreds engendered by lack of political acumen, does not upgrade us as much as it downgrades those whose job it is to represent us realistically, with sounder knowledge of the land and its people. Will Rogers said he had never met a man he didn't like. He could have added that with some he had to try harder than with others.

Principally for her devoted comradeship during the Memphis experience and the days there when she would have preferred the cleanliness and quiet of her Washington life, in requiem to Memphis here is a bit of my wife's cogent text on that vanished city. Secondarily, I offer it because I am incapable of conveying the mental image as she has done. Quoted here are the final pages of her monograph on Memphis.

"Memphis recedes into obscurity in the chronicle of history. There is no doubt but that it continued as a thickly-populated and prosperous city although it had ceased to be the great metropolis and the residence of kings. Its situation on the Nile made it the center of trade for all the produce of the country and for international commerce as well. But all of Egypt suffered from the heavy hand of Rome and its ever growing exaction of money and of food. Egypt became the granary of Rome, and under the increasing and impossible burden of producing more and more, in crops and in gold, sank into complete degeneration. Internal trouble between the Romans, the Greeks, the Jews and the Egyptians helped to hasten the decline. We pass over these early centuries of the Christian era in Egypt. Our story is of Memphis and no history was written of its dying days.

"Helpless and defenseless Egypt was exposed to the inroads of barbarians and in 639 A.D. was conquered by the Mohammedans. (Petrie declares that the Roman governor signed the capitulation to the Mohammedans in the palace of Memphis.) In 641 their leader Amr founded his capital city, Fostat (which later became Cairo), on the east bank of the Nile a few miles north of Memphis. The buildings, the mosques, and the walls of the new city were constructed of materials plundered from Memphis. Temples and palaces were razed, monuments broken up and burned to produce lime, statues and ornaments transported from the ancient city to the new. Memphis became a quarry and was not spared by the reckless hands of the barbarians, and with its stone and timber went its rights and privileges and honor.

"After 4,000 years of glory and distinction, Memphis was dead. The "City of the White Wall" had lived through many wars and sieges. It was said that the armies of foreign invaders through the centuries never regarded Egypt as conquered until Memphis had fallen. Always she had risen again, great and powerful as before. But this time the destruction, the dismemberment and mutilation were complete. The final conquest of Memphis, the execution of the city, had been achieved by the Mohammedans.

"The ruins of Memphis had no equal. Even in death, Memphis retained beauty and distinction. Its remains have commanded awe and admiration from countless generations of travelers. In 1162 a great scholar was born in Baghdad. He traveled extensively and taught medicine and philosophy in Cairo and Damascus. He was one of the circle of learned men whom Saladin gathered around him in Jerusalem. In his work 'An Account of Egypt' (Bodleian Library, Oxford), Abd-Al Latif describes the ruins of Memphis:

> 'Enormous as are the extent and antiquity of this city, in spite of the frequent change of governments whose yoke it has borne, and the great pains more than one nation has been at to destroy it, to sweep its last trace from the face of the earth, to carry away the stones and materials of which it was constructed, to mutilate the statues which adorned it; in spite, finally, of all that more than 4,000 years have done in addition to man, these ruins still offer to the eye of the beholder a mass of marvels which bewilder the senses and which the most skillful pens must fail to describe. The more deeply we contemplate this city the more our admiration rises and every fresh glance at the ruins is a fresh source of delight.'

"Abd-Al Latif describes with indignation and contempt the thirst for gold of his contemporaries, calling it a disease; and the systematic search of the ruins by treasure-seekers. This disease was endemic in Memphis throughout the centuries until at last the plundered ruins could yield no more.—Even the ruins disappeared.

"After the extinction of the city followed the encroachment of nature, ably abetted by man. The mud brick of temple walls became his hovel. The soil was rich where the city had stood. His date palms flourished and he planted more. His crops throve, fertilized by sebakh (the saline dust of decomposing brick) and he extended his cultivation. Rural tranquility replaced the stir of the metropolis and the fruit of the soil rather than the treasuries of kings became the wealth of Memphis.

"Today it is well nigh impossible, even for one with the keenest imagination, to visualize the fabulous city. The pastoral scene stretches north, south, east and west. Everywhere there is quiet motion, the fellah with his donkeys, camels, water buffalo, going

Memphis

and coming in ceaseless slow activity. Thousands of date palms exhibit their beauty and their burden of fruit far overhead in the gentle breeze. Women do their washing in the still pond where the West Gate of the Temple of Ptah once raised its splendid pillars to the sky. Children wade and play around the broken fragments which lie half submerged in the shallow water.

"Occasionally a cloud of dust signals the approach of an automobile or bus on the road from Bad Rashein to Sakkara. They may bring tourists but their stay will be brief. There is so little to see. The colossal statue of Rameses II, lying in state in its shelter, awesome and stately despite its lack of legs, is the chief point of interest. A few hundred yards away a smaller Rameses statue lay on the ground in a grove of palms. This year it was removed to Cairo to become a permanent exhibit in the station plaza. How many of the hurrying millions will pause to glance at Rameses there?

"Directly to the east and only a few paces from the shed of the colossus an alabaster sphinx of great beauty and timeless dignity rests on its pedestal. One hears rumors that Cairo is casting covetous eyes upon it also—twentieth-century plunderers! Across the dusty road a small stela with the head of the goddess Hathor is half hidden in the weeds. Nearby a small sanctuary of Seti I has been partially and badly reconstructed. To the west another small sanctuary, this one of Rameses II, was recently excavated.

"Here the eye is gratified although the mind protests the seeping water which rises and falls around its broken columns. The magnificent alabaster altar or libation table in what was the embalming house of the Apis bull remains in situ, in perfect condition. How its beauty escaped the tools of the despoilers through the ages is a mystery. Its lovely proportions and the skill with which it was wrought inspire one with respectful admiration for its ancient creators.

"There is little else to see of the city of which it was said in a late period long after decay and ruin had set in that 'it was half a day's journey to walk through it from north to south.' Excavated sections of mud and brick walls, broken fragments of stelae and columns, potsherds, a bit of ancient paving—nothing more remains. Only a person with an objective and interest would cross the fields and irrigation ditches and sandy tracts to the site where the Palace of Apries once towered above the city.

"But he who does so is rewarded; not by the climb to the top of the surviving remnants of the massive mud brick walls, nor by the broken parts of column capitals scattered about. Reward comes in a sudden infinitesimal perception of what used to be. Perhaps it is the elevation and the wide panorama, the great valley of the Nile extending mile after verdant mile to the north and south. Beyond the river to the east is the Mokattam range of bare limestone hills where the stone for palaces and pyramids was quarried 5,000 years ago.

"Finally to the west stretches the great plateau of the Libyan desert crowned with its pyramids and mastaba tombs. Giza, Abousir, Sakkara, Dahshur—they cover twenty miles but the eyes strain to see farther for there are more. This was the great necropolis of Memphis and these are the monuments of the mighty, the Pharaohs, the nobles, the high priests, the generals, who made Memphis the greatest city of antiquity. The desert preserved their tombs; man destroyed their city. Memphis has disappeared. This is written in commemoration, with reverence and affection for the noble city and with hope that these words may, in a small way, help to keep alive the memory of its ancient brilliance."

The Boat Grave of Cheops

FOUR THOUSAND years ago is light exercise to the geologist or student of this world's past behavior. The Gulf Stream and the Humboldt Current, uncharted and unnamed, had been developing their energies at the same source, creating the same climatic conditions, supporting the same sea life as they had for millions of years. Glacial chunks were sliding from the same icy slopes of Greenland and floating unseen into the huge basin of the North Atlantic where its increasing warmth absorbed them into its salty vastness. Winds with their cargoes of moisture crashed against the nearest uplands, depositing their rains then, unburdened, vaulted their heights to bleach less fortunate areas to leeward into lifeless deserts.

But on the Nile four thousand years ago it was then the late Stone Age. The river people were making rafts of bundled reeds. The same ageless breeze was blowing from the north, contrary to the flow of the river's silty waters. Motive energy for moving upstream came from the sail. Downstream sails were furled and the mighty current powered vessels northward at varying speeds, depending upon flood or low water.

As it was in the early days of the Pharaonic period so it is today. The single-winged felucca opens its broad, loose-footed sail to the north wind and bucks the current tirelessly during the daylight hours, anchoring or mooring at night as the wind dies, to preserve its hard-earned miles. Downstream the long-bladed rudder guides the heavy craft, sail furled, past the treacherous sand bars and shallow spots, with a serpentine recklessness. Crews and families live aboard, often for weeks, as they traverse hundreds of monotonous miles. The gods of ancient Egypt were numerous and of major and minor importance. But the River was actual and practical and outranked them all. To glide regally over its sacred waters, boats of a hundred feet and longer were maintained by the Pharaohs and men of means. When King Menes, a southerner, combined southern and northern Egypt under his single crown he moved in state down the Nile by royal boat to receive his coronation. Boat transportation was the modus operandi for the living, the ritual for the dead.

Boat graves are not uncommon near the pyramids of Giza. Some graves contain the remains of smaller craft which obviously represented nothing more than token transport. Abdel Moneim Abubakr, former Professor of Egyptology at the University of Cairo, quotes the Pyramid Texts, "The reed floats of Heaven are placed for the King Pep, as he crosses by means of them to the horizon and Ra." Abubakr goes on to say that this passage and its many variants shows us that the deceased king was in need of a vessel to ferry him across the sky in order to reach the place where his father the sun god dwelt.

But the discovery at Giza in 1954 contained a real boat, a river-plowing one, a royal yacht which created some justification for the excitement and international headlines it engendered. The discovery, as has so often been the case in Egypt, was accidental. Workmen had been put to clearing accumulated debris from the south side of the Great pyramid. The heavy layer consisted of small broken rock, remains of the original pyramid casing, lost long ago, and windblown sand. (The modern archaeologist scrupulously examines and even takes soundings of proposed dumping ground to prevent double handling.) At ground or rock level these workmen came upon a row of massive stones, well cut and lying with only their top sides exposed. Further clearing revealed a row of rectangular blocks stretching close to a hundred feet.

Members of the Egyptian Antiquities Department were alerted by Salah Osman, engineer member in charge of the clearing work. Workmen were shunted aside and every stone was tenderly brushed clean in search of clues to dating and Pharaonic connection. The scholars were convinced that the stones covered a long pit and that the pit contained a boat—unmolested, they prayed. Finally on the last stone to the eastward, after carefully removing the lime dust, they spotted the painted name of Radedef, son and successor of Cheops, whose resting place was in the largest of all the pyramids. Radedef had also brought his father's boat from the river—not just a puny replica or symbolic affair—and had it buried beside him.

With understandable impatience one of the Department members ordered a corner of one of the huge roof stones cut away just enough to admit a man's head. After all, there was little need for further effort if the grave were empty or if its contents had been wrecked centuries before. After two days the hole was made and an electric bulb lowered on a long cord. The members of the Department in turn looked upon the lime-dust-covered deck of the royal boat of Cheops, undisturbed since its interment some forty-five hundred years before.

Teena was there that morning and, after the VIPs and I had knelt over awkwardly for a look, Teena was asked to be the first lady to behold the boat. Women did not wear slacks in those days in Egypt and I am sure the men present thought that the necessary bottoms-up posture would deter her. But they did not know my Teena. She tucked her skirts tightly behind her knees and was over the hole unabashed. Later when the first flash pictures were taken through the hole, Salah Osman gave her a copy which she has today.

The world press quickly picked up the story, glamorizing it with inaccuracies and impulsive theorizing. The buildup was unhealthy and transformed into a cause célèbre what to sophisticated Egyptian historians would have been just another if somewhat larger boat grave. Jealousies developed over such trivial questions as who found the boat grave, who first saw it and other such minutiae. One high-placed member of the Department was fired for lecturing on the boat and pronouncing himself the real discoverer.

Dr. Abubakr was thrown into this cauldron of hot-blooded rivalry, with orders to uncover the boat by lifting some forty massive limestone blocks—weights unknown at that time, but which ranged up to twenty tons per stone. Then, the boat exposed, further consultations would be held to decide how it would be removed and treated or vice versa. Abubakr's responsibility was awesome. If he succeeded, the project would be catagorized as routine. If he failed, if for any cause one of those behemoths fell in process of lifting and wrecked the precious boat, the fault and instant disgrace would be his.

The young engineer, Salah Osman, was then employed by the Department of Antiquities as surveyor and maintenance man for the ruins thereabouts. Abubakr engaged him and a capable foreman to build a scaffolding and install lifting apparatus over the grave. One ordinary twenty-ton crane, common equipment for modern construction elsewhere, would have solved the problem. There would have *been* no problem: But Osman had no crane, no prospects of one. He would use what he had or could accumulate by scraping through the poorly-stocked depots of the Government. Courage and raw skills were to be his implements.

Every stone, until lifted and examined by the experts, must be considered a treasure. The mere wrapping of a hemp line around it could obliterate paint, brittle with age but displaying graffiti, quarry marks, even cartouches or identification marks.

The workmen collected and stacked timber and planking at the grave site. The largest timbers 12"x12" were laid as sills along the sides of the boat chamber. Next, strongly built A frames were assembled by the carpenters, inverted and erected along the sills at twelve foot intervals, and braced there with random lumber. Osman and his crew then fastened heavy beams or stringers across the flat tops of the A frames. The beam lumber had been used many times before for miscellaneous purposes and required constant splicing. Where possible the splices were gauged to fit over the A frames for strength.

Once the frames were in place and the stringers fastened, steel rails, formerly used for hauling debris from the excavations to the dumping ground, were lifted by the men and firmly spiked to the stringers, creating a track of about ten feet gauge. Next they disassembled a dump cart, salvaging its wheels and axles. Upon those they constructed a dolly of sturdy timbers. The broad gauge of the track would provide a wide purchase on the stones and reduce turning or side motion.

From some undisclosed source those resourceful men produced two hand-operated chain hoists. These they suspended, with much rattling of chains, from the dolly by several turns of well-seasoned, five strand, one and one half inch manila-type rope. The dolly would move along from above one stone to another, the hoists lifting each stone in turn, whereupon the dolly, rolling on, would carry its burden to the far end of the grave and lower it onto heavy skids. From there each stone would be levered beyond the working area. This was the theory. Would it work?

It was then that I was offered my bit part in this drama, one that had never been produced before and for which there could be no rehearsal. It was to be a part in which I never appeared, like the offstage voice of Mr. Magoo, a minor deus ex machina. My studies at the Embalming House at Mit Rahineh were behind me. My chores as Director were reduced to the monotony of procurement of supplies and funds, and maintaining friendly intercourse with our Arab counterparts while wrangling for our promised equipment.

This spectacular exhumation of the boat, and the makeshift method of its recovery, was about to take place practically within view from our hotel window in Cairo! It intrigued me. I went to the site at every opportunity to witness the construction. Salah Osman gave Teena and me each a pass to the fenced-off site which allowed us to wander over the grave area at will.

One morning Professor Abubakr asked Teena and me to lunch at his home nearby in the desert. After lunch he and I adjourned to his terrace for coffee. He spoke to me in a tone uncommon for an Egyptian addressing an American. I liked Abubakr and he knew it. I realized the strain the man was undergoing, of the rivalries, almost hatreds, foolishly generated by the boat.

"Mr. Dimick," he asked, "How would you have done this job with what we had?"

"Professor," I answered, "I couldn't do it." "But," he continued, "You have watched the erection of this lifting mechanism. You realize that just one weakness undetected could destroy it all. Yet this is the structure, along with its components, which I must trust." Here was a fine man, one whom Teena and I had grown to respect, left with no alternative. He must go forward.

"Professor," I volunteered, "Why don't I go over the entire structure, using my American and other tables of stresses and strains and weights, and write you a report?" I will not say that he seemed grateful, just relieved. It was agreed that I would start the following day.

On the way back to Cairo that afternoon my ever-protecting wife uttered, "Heaven forbid that it falls now; we Americans woud be blamed 'til eternity." She really did not fear that ending or anticipate it. Neither did I.

Next morning I arrived at the boat grave. It was then just two weeks prior to the well-publicized date for lifting the first stone. Already the carpenters were erecting a shed over the scaffolding and a tier of seats at one end. There the VIPs would gather along with reporters and broadcasters from over the world. They would witness the lifting of the first stone and give the story to the Egyptians and to the outside world.

I had my permit for unlimited access and began by crawling in and out among the frames and track twenty feet above the blocks. By the end of that morning I had my notes and was ready to turn to my manuals for guidance. Two days later I handed Professor Abubakr a copy of my findings. I had actually finished it in two hours, maybe less, but the fear of some miscalculation obsessed me to a point where, after a ridiculous amount of re-checking, I still hesitated to surrender my written words. Here is a condensed copy of the report, eliminating only some of the burdensome technicalities:-

Memphis

Memorandum to Prof. Abubakr

Furthering our recent discussion concerning the stone blocks covering the boat grave at Giza and present plans for lifting them, here are some thoughts on the engineering problems involved. My analysis is based entirely upon the methods you are now committed to for lifting the stones, not on how it could be done if proper and adequate equipment were available.

First let me comment on the sound, if elementary, physics which has gone into the job. In that connection I compliment Mr. Osman and his crew for what they have accomplished with what was on hand or accessible. In addition to his utter loyalty Mr. Osman possesses some primary essentials of a good engineer: desire for absolute performance, and great caution. My association with him is pleasant and rewarding. Now to my calculations:-

We are concerned only with the weight of the heaviest stone while preparing for the lifting and removal of all of them, frictional breakaway resistance being considered equal. My measurements of what appears to be the largest block are 4.50 x 1.80 x .85 meters. That block would contain 6.88 cu. meters. Listed below are the sources consulted for weights of limestone, together with their calculations. Variations no doubt result from differences in quality of limestone in separated areas.

Source	Maximum lbs. per cu. meter	Weight of block at 6.88 cu. m.	
U.S. Eng. Handbook	6,020	41,400	Approx.
O'Rourke Eng. Handbook	5,900	40,600	”
Eshbach, Eng. Fundamentals	6,390	44,000	”
Archie, St. Eng. Tables	4,600	31,600	”
		157,600	

Average weight 39,400 lbs. or approx. 40,000 lbs., 20 tons.

In the interest of good practice let us add a factor of safety of fifty percent and consider our heaviest block to weigh 30 tons and base our calculations on that figure in dealing with the various components of the lifting equipment.

ROPE

Manila-type hemp rope is on hand in quantity. It is one-and-one-half inch, five strand, in good condition. The international formula for breaking point of this rope is 7000 lbs. x D^2 in inches + 600 lbs. Translated to the rope on hand we have 7000 x 2.25 + 600 = 16,350 pounds per turn of rope, approximately 8 tons. Two turns provide 16 tons pull on each of the two chain hoists. The hoist hooks are broad and deep and can easily hold three turns.

HOISTS

Two hand-operated worm-gear hoists are on hand and will be used in conjunction. Each is of 20 tons capacity, the figure stamped on the gear housing. Common practice of the manufacturer provides large safety factors for equipment of this nature and it is conservative to say that capacities when new were at least 25 tons. My inspection disclosed no wear or defects in either hoist.

SCAFFOLDING

I was not present during the entire fabrication and erection of the scaffolding but I have since examined the A frames. Timbers, while not of prime stock, appear to be sound, and the method of erection is in line with good practice. Splices, when required in the stringers, have been placed over the A frames whenever possible. In other cases the splices have been fortified by a lateral timber securely bolted over the joint. Actual stress resistance of such a splice depends directly upon the bolts. I consider them equal to the stress expected.

TRACK

The rail for the track is lighter than would have been selected, were heavier available. A more desirable weight would have been at least 40 pounds per yard. However, the lighter rail has been well spiked to the stringers and should not buckle or turn. Its low crown should aid in preventing critical misbehavior.

DOLLY

The carriage has been well built on 1⅜" steel axles which revolve in forged roller bearing stuffing boxes. The chassis consists of two 15" x 15" timbers, bolted at right angles to the axles. Those in turn support two cross timbers of the same dimensions. This method spreads the area of down thrust to a maximum and produces a safety factor too large to warrant calculation. The two hoists will be suspended from the dolly by turns of the same quality and size of rope as described under that heading.

By the foregoing process we have proceeded upward from the gravity-bound blocks of limestone through the equipment assembled for their removal. A good job has been done by your crew. It should be noted that no allowance has been made in this report for kinetic or static friction. Those factors are indeterminate until tested. It is my understanding that friction will be relieved on stone number one by sawing between it and the next one. After that the problem with the others should be negligible. It is wise here to say a word about press releases concerning the boat. I assure you that your Department will be respected by me in all such matters. It will only be necessary for me to report to my two sponsors, the University of Pennsylvania Museum and the American Research Center in Cairo, both of which are in contact with you and your Department of Antiquities.

Signed,
JOHN DIMICK

Two small wedge stones of four or five hundred pounds each at the very west end of the pit served to fill the irregular end of the opening. These were removed. Holes were drilled between the first and second blocks and the ropes dangled through the holes. From the wedge opening men could reach under and bring the rope around and over. Repetition of this provided as many turns of the rope as required. At precisely 10:20 on the morning of November 23, 1954, the westernmost stone of the grave roof responded to the tug of the two chain hoists and slowly rose and hung suspended over the rectangular gap. A preliminary speech by the Minister of Education contained the usual glorifications. Now the climax was past. A heavy, musty perfume rose from the dark interior. Reporters gathered to ask their questions. Bill Downes, then as now a noted correspondent, approached me while I stood by Osman. "Dimick, what did you have to do with this affair?" he asked. It was comforting that I could answer, "Nothing," whereupon I introduced him to Osman.

Thus pass the incidents that are without incident. The remaining stones came away without difficulty, some more reluctantly than others, until the entire boat lay corpselike in the crypt. The pit measured 101' x 8' 4" x 11' 3" deep, but only the actual hull of the boat fitted into it. The long bowsprit, terminating in the shape of a giant papyrus, had been cruelly removed at burial time and stacked grotesquely on deck. The boat was braced against the pit sides with planking and part of a steering oar. All topside gear, mast, etc., had been lowered and placed on deck. Lines and what may have been extra caulking were there in surprising preservation.

Much has been written about the boat since its discovery and exposure. The efforts to remove and reassemble it were long, disorganized and ineffectual. Abubakr and Osman moved on, unacclaimed but unscathed, to other ventures in their land of unending adventure. I went back to my part at Memphis.

Tikal

It was the summer of 1955. Our lungs and scalps were barely purged of the last grains of desert sand and Memphis silt. My name had made the list inside the back cover of the Museum's publication "Expedition" under Research Associates. It felt good there, though shivering timidly in its unlettered nakedness among all those M.S.s, B.S.s and Ph.Ds.

We were battling my sixth, seventh or eighth ulcer. But for the X-rays, which disclosed another island of scar tissue, it was pure guess work in those years of gastronomic misery if the cavity was new or just an old one, reopened and antagonized by premature return to cocktails, tobacco and stupid fretting.

One morning in Washington, a note came from Eugenia Madeira. She was inviting us for dinner and the night the following week at Crumdale, their farm west of Philadelphia. Percy had digestive problems, too. I could join him, if necessary, in his soft, bland and disgusting diet. But my sympathetic and indulgent doctor had again reluctantly agreed to a mild cessation of restrictions for the week to come, so we accepted.

We arrived at Crumdale in time to change. The dinner guest list provided a clue which I should not have missed, but did. Everyone was connected in some way with the Museum. Percy the Chairman, Froelich Rainey the Director, the other male guests all members of the Board. Percy's house boasts a chiminea, one of those beckoning walk-in fireplace affairs with chairs and sofas around a wood fire which burns unfettered on the stone floor in the center. The smoke, under perfect control, rises languidly into the high funnel-shaped chimney.

Presently we were men only in the chiminea, unusual for cocktails. A few moments and two bourbons later I called Teena to the door. "Dear, they want me to organize a restoration of Tikal. I think I said 'yes,' depending on you." Teena searched my expression for any obvious results of my empty glass. She was too well aware of my latest battle of the duodenum. Even the most otherwise tranquil domestic climates are affected by ulcers in the male. But Teena saw my almost childish excitement. "If you feel up to it, do accept by all means." I would have deliberated longer had I known it meant five years, but my answer would have been the same.

"*Place where spirit voices are heard*"

Teobert Maler in his accounts of his visit to Tikal, in northern Guatemala, published in 1904, gives that ghostly translation from the Maya. Another less eerie paraphrasing gives "TI" to mean to whisper and "KAL" the throat or esophagus. Thus Tikal, whispering voices. Often today the descendants who live in those lands speak of their ancestors returning, dressed in their former regalia, to revisit their temples where their spirit voices are heard high among the trees.

Tikal proper covered perhaps four square miles. Its environs and satellite villages ranged miles further into the jungle of the Peten. That prodigious rain forest ranks among the massive ones of the western hemisphere. Jaguars, monkeys, constrictors and tropical birds abound, while varieties of orchids literally clutter the trees.

No one knows when man first came to Tikal, certainly he was there two thousand years before Christ. His building skills and some cultures advanced steadily. But those accentuated his lack of other accomplishments which would seem far less difficult to modern man.

J. Eric Thompson in his *Rise and Fall of Maya Civilization* lists some intellectual idiosyncrasies:

    They charted the heavens yet failed to grasp the principle of the wheel.

    They visualized eternity but ignored the short step from the corbeled arch to true arch.

    They could count in millions yet never learned to weigh a sack of corn.

Those were the people who built Tikal in ever progressing stages of splendor until it became immortalized in its Late Classic Period, five hundred years before Columbus.

Tikal, like all great Maya cities, was the ceremonial center, the court for social and religious congregation, the Holy City, the market place, the arena for games. The population lived in earthen-floored huts around it, the Vatican surrounded by Rome, Its steadily building accretion was instance of the population explosion among its worshipers.

Tikal declined languorously into its fall and destruction. Its people spread farther and farther afield in search of fresh lands to cultivate. Protection by its faithful was dissipated by their remoteness. Vandal tribes, always lurking nearby, found resistance diminishing. They moved on the city slowly but inexorably. There is no account of a battle for Tikal, or of it falling by quick enemy surge. Pride of possession lessened, upkeep dwindled, and, in its slow but insidious fashion, nature began to reclaim and smother the once lordly city. By the fourteenth century it was deserted. Only the name endured. Again the ghosts were whispering.

The chicken or the egg—do we start hiring and hope for success with our drive for funds or should we have at least a small stake before embarking upon a million dollar job in the jungle? Tikal was going to be a lucky job; the answer was handed to us. Edwin M. Shook was available as field director. Although he was not released entirely by Carnegie Institution he would soon be one of those to go when that body completed the dissolution of its archaeological section. Ed knew Tikal and Guatemala. He loved them both. He agreed to become field director. Next the money.

Honest enthusiasm for an idea distills a disbelief that all those approached for help will not share it. Certainly foundations will leap at the chance to finance Tikal, be offended if not invited. My awakening was to be harsh.

We drew on our meager Museum nest egg to send Shook ahead. We had to have photographs and a story to sell the venture. Rainey and Madeira were game. We could draw on old reports for the history of Tikal. Then my first break came, and like most breaks, I had made it myself, but unwittingly, years before.

In 1947, in Guatemala City, a polite note had come to my hotel. "Dear Mr. Dimick: Could you dine with Mrs. Mellon and me tonight or tomorrow night?" signed Matthew Mellon. We met that night. Mrs. Mellon was an energetic Germanic type. Dr. Mellon was slight and a bit older. Over cocktails Dr. Mellon came to the point promptly. Mrs. Mellon had heard of Tikal and wanted to see it. What could I tell her about how to reach the ruins?

Her enthusiasm was obvious, as was his lack of it. He was

not going. Addressing myself to her I laid out the procedure step by step. "First, Mrs. Mellon, you hire a jeep here, no other car can negotiate the road. If the jeep is in good condition and the driver reliable, you should reach Flores in a long day, six A.M. to nightfall. There is a rickety plane to Flores about once a week which picks up chicle, but it is not too dependable, bucket seats and no seatbelts. You can spend the night in a small pension at Flores. Have your insect powder always in hand. You will have brought your sleeping bag, food and supplies with you. Next morning you hire two Indians and three mules. One man will be your guide, the other cook and general helper. The Peten rain forest is trackless in spots. If your guide is competent and lucky in not getting temporarily lost several times, you should reach Tikal after two nights. A day to see the ruins, a night there, then two nights back to Flores. The Indians will not be harmful, but neither are they very brilliant conversationalists. May I suggest, Mrs. Mellon, that within a year or so there will be a short airstrip very near Tikal, adequate for landing a small plane. Wait for that; you could go and come in a day."

Much of the tiger had left Mrs. Mellon by now. She decided to wait, and Dr. Mellon showed his relief. In a moment alone after dinner he thanked me and hoped that some day he could do something in return. Would I like to go next month on his yacht with some ornithologists to the Galapagos? "No thanks."

By 1955 the Scaiffe Foundation, Sarah Mellon Scaiffe, was growing into real importance. It was a Pennsylvania foundation, why not try? But our first introduction to the Foundation must be impressive — Dr. Mellon was Mrs. Scaiffe's first cousin. From the Savoy Plaza in New York I called his office in Pittsburgh. Dr. Mellon was in New York, leaving for Europe the following day. "Where in New York?" I inquired. "The Savoy Plaza," came the electrifying answer.

Dr. Mellon was in when I called, and remembered me. "Where are you?" he asked.

"2107."

"Well, I am in 2210, could you come up?"

I bounded up the one flight. His room was in the usual disarray preceding a sailing. "Dr. Mellon, I know you must be very busy, so let me come to the point: I want to meet your cousin, Sarah Scaiffe." He waited for me to say more. No doubt he expected me to remind him of his wish to do something for me in return for Guatemala. He seemed pleased when it was not mentioned. "The Museum plans to restore parts of Tikal. I believe we could interest Mrs. Scaiffe if I could talk with her."

He took a sheet of Savoy Plaza stationery from the desk and wrote "Dear Cousin Sarah:" — The letter was flattering but I loved it. We parted soon after. I contacted the Scaiffe Foundation and Mr. and Mrs. Scaiffe personally with my hopes and plans, then we at the Museum waited. In a month or so Mr. Scaiffe called from New York (my lucky city). "Could someone from the Museum come up for further talk about Tikal?" We sent Ted Kidder, son of Dr. A. V. Kidder and associate director of the Museum. We thought it wiser at that juncture to send someone high up in the Museum. Three weeks later we received $75,000.00 from the Scaiffe Foundation! Tikal project was off the ground; that first olive was out of the bottle.

Aubrey Trik was anxious to return to archaeology. He came to us after two years in commercial architecture, as restoration expert and assistant to Shook. William Coe, long a Maya scholar at the University, became chief archaeologist. The roster swelled with names of eager specialists who had long hoped to see Tikal systematically undertaken. Teena and I went down to get a new feel of the site before I embarked on the fund raising.

Shook had already commandeered some deserted shacks built by the Guatemala Air Force at a time when the Honduras unpleasantness was seething. The huts were near the airstrip and

TIKAL   Temple I cleared of heavy brush and trees.

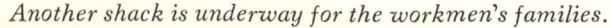

Clearing camp site; Note partially completed shack in background.

Another shack is underway for the workmen's families.

A DC-3 brings supplies to Tikal.

Kerosene operated appliances were installed before shacks were built.

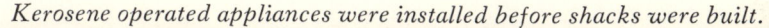

Above: The medic examines a worker's eye. He also doubled as a school teacher—first in the Tikal area.

Top Right: A section from a huge Peten tree becomes lumber.

Bottom Right: Finished houses.

First potable water, distilled from the stagnant water in the swamp at rear.

Above: A divided reservoir showing one part covered to reduce evaporation and the one in the foreground open. Shading was later discontinued because of algae formation.

Following Pages: Main plaza of Tikal today looking north over palace group; Temple I is at right, Temple II to the left and the north concourse in middle background.

Temple I grubbed to disclose terraces and stairway in center.

Pipe scaffolding was erected to restore top of Temple I.

Above: From this and similar quarries the ancient Maya cut their stone. Our restoration materials were taken from the same pits.

Top Right: A smaller platform which was cleared and used to develop Indians into masons who would later work on the large temples.

Bottom Right: Trial temple restored after numerous mistakes by trainees. Most of them went on to become excellent masons.

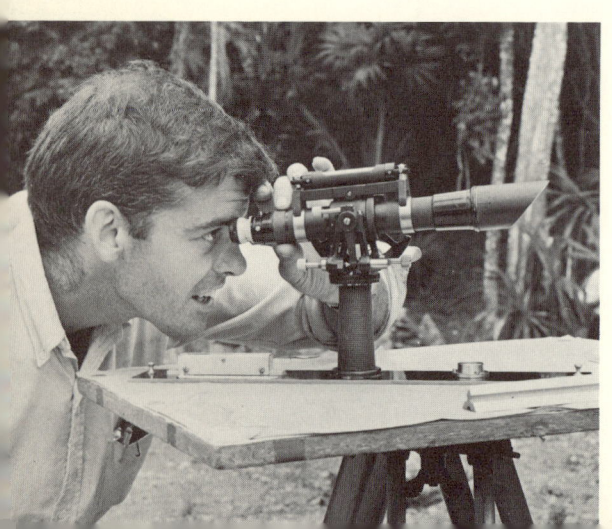

Above: This enormous exploratory pit dug by William R. Coe traced Tikal occupation back to 600 B.C.

Left: Bill Coe at work on the plane table.

A. S. Trik in process of cleaning and recording the contents of the huge tomb he discovered under Temple I. Some 16 pounds of carved jade adorned the lone occupant. Near the skull is an earplug of jade, while around the neck is a tubular necklace of jade. The large jade balls in the foreground formed a girdle.

Temple I dominates the main plaza of Tikal. Temple II is in the foreground.

became our first headquarters. Air transportation was going to be extremely expensive unless something could be done. Again a lucky solution developed. Guatemala's President could promise no money, but he was enthusiastic. The Air Force would fly us and our supplies from Puerto Barrios, on the east coast, or Guatemala City. Thousands of dollars were to be saved. Right away planes started dropping in with bags of corn and beans, canned goods, all of them heavy items. Small tools which had been lying in Guatemala for days now dropped out of the sky at our feet. Later trucks and bulldozers would be dismantled and also brought by air, even a sawmill. The Museum could buy heavy machinery at special discounts in Philadelphia, but ocean freight was a big cost item. United Fruit had certainly made its full contribution to me at Zaculeu, but when I asked the Company to carry our heavy items from the States to Puerto Barrios free, it agreed; up to four tons per voyage, a big donation.

Teena and I arrived in Tikal to find things humming. A bulldozer and a truck had been dismantled in Barrios, flown in and reassembled. Men were busily lengthening the airstrip. Material and supplies were strewn over the ground, dumped hastily by the Guatemala Air Force.

Shook had native workmen building temporary huts with their one tool, the machete, a versatile implement in their hands. They cut small trees in quantities and hauled them into camp. With the same tool they dug holes into the hard limestone for corner posts, then dropped the clean straight poles in and secured them upright with small chunks of stone. When those were set, if the hut was to have sides they lashed horizontal poles to them by binding the corners with strong vines brought from the jungle.

They packed mud between the poles, lathering it by hand. Next the roofcomb was raised and knotted to sides with smaller branches and more vines to form a tent-like framework. The palm leaves had been saved and separated into fanlike clusters. These were laid over the roof framework in artistic fashion until the entire roof was a solid mass of palm fronds six inches or more thick. It was impervious to rain and effective protection against the sun. Four men would build a shack like this, twenty feet by ten feet, in two days. Mosquito netting covered the windows or hung over each hammock. The door could be a piece of framed burlap. Hammocks were strung between the posts, and this was home for the crew for the first season.

The workers had started clearing the great plaza. Teena looked up at that handsome temple which guarded the plaza on the east, 135 feet tall. "Why can't I do something?" she asked. "I want to underwrite the restoration of this building." Our second break had come. We were a long way from the million dollar estimate, but we had impetus. I collected my photographs and story into an improvised brochure and returned to the U.S.A. My weapon was in hand, now whom to attack?

It was to be a long siege and a frustrating one. Ford Foundation was politely adamant. "Sorry, not in our line." Then Rockefeller Foundation. Certainly that body would react favorably. Two years later I had littered the files of that otherwise immaculate body with history, photographs and progress reports of Tikal, without a penny in return or slight hope for one.

Dean Rusk, President of the Foundation, had exceeded his usual forbearance by giving me personal appointments almost whenever I asked, or within a day or so. Once, when his calendar was jammed, he even let me come for coffee before his official day began. He favored Tikal Project but his Directors, like Ford's, had ruled out archaeology. Advancement of health and education all over the world were quite enough of an undertaking even for Rockefeller Foundation.

Dean Rusk finally had to tell me, as gently as possible — "John, we have twenty-one members on our Board, nineteen are against you. Personally I am in favor. In some instances the Board allows me to give up to ten thousand dollars on my own judgment. You may have the full amount for Tikal."

"Sorry", I said. "I can't accept. My project would be damned by faint praise. If Rockefeller gives me only ten thousand dollars toward a needed eight hundred thousand, where do I turn for the important money? Of course I cannot refuse it without the Museum's consent, but I must strongly recommend against it."

I called Percy Madeira from there. Percy, being the keen banker he was, overrode me on the sound premise that this way we at least had a start with the Foundation. His mature judgment was later to bear fruit.

While in New York, a fairly reliable grapevine told me that the Avalon Foundation had recently been "beefed up," parlance for receiving new funds from its founders. Dr. Thomas Parran was President. The Foundation was the creation of Mrs. Ailsa Mellon Bruce. The Mellons would soon think I had no other source for funds, but the two were separate and distinct. I called Dr. Parran and got an appointment. The Foundation's handsome offices occupied a small stone home on upper Park Avenue. Dr. Parran received me at twelve and suggested lunch at a little restaurant he liked in the neighborhood. It was relaxing, talking over the martinis which Dr. Parran suggested. I told him our needs, what we had in hand, and answered his educated questions.

"What have you in mind from Avalon, Mr. Dimick?" If he noticed my hesitation he did not reveal it.

"Dr. Parran, we would like $150,000.00, fifty thousand a year for three years."

He did not seem at all overawed. "The project seems worthy to me. Our Board meets in about two weeks and I think I can recommend it. I will need a formal request from your Museum at an early date. Usually our Board depends upon me in matters of this nature."

In three weeks we had the hoped-for letter from Dr. Parran, "Request acted upon favorably." We were off to our goal, past the mid-point and well down the stretch.

The following season Mrs. Scaiffe came to Tikal, liked what

she saw and approved what her first donation had accomplished. She promised additional help, which arrived shortly after. Our exchequer was growing now under its own impetus. Visitors who came volunteered small gifts. Our annual gifts of five hundred dollars and under were approaching ten thousand dollars. Miss Alice Tully came to see the ruins. A small temple on the north side intrigued her. "Could I underwrite that structure?" she asked. The fact that she is my adored sister-in-law had nothing to do with the alacrity of my acceptance. On another visit, when we needed an additional automatic dump cart, she said in her modest fashion, "Perhaps I could arrange that." Such occurrences proved the impact which Tikal had on all who came. It was selling itself.

How does one describe Alice Tully and maintain credibility with the listener, especially to another woman? She is first a man's woman. A woman of exquisite femininity but who, in street shoes, climbed a volcano on Santorini strewn with razor-edged chunks of obsidian, just to be closer to its crater, inhale its restless sulphur fumes, and meditate its past fury. It is difficult to associate one of America's great patrons of the arts, music, painting and sculpture, with a woman whose passion and love for animal life takes her to Ethiopia just to make friends with and pet Selassie's lion, who takes a giant boa in her hands and allows it around her neck. Alice possesses an enviable combination of tenderness, discrimination and fearlessness.

But it was the last quality which was so painfully tested on a moonlit night at Tikal. We were just a small group that night, no tourists, when Ed Shook suggested that we return to the great plaza and experience the eerie effects of moonlight and soft shadows. The full moon over Tikal is alive. Curtains of ephemeral white puffy clouds, as they float by, give it the illusion of gentle movement as it tiptoes along the topmost branches of the giant ceibas, the sacred trees of the Maya. Departing the forests, its light probes the plaza floor, silently traversing it like a big jungle cat on the prowl, until it climbs the trees on the opposite side as the moon continues its pageantry in their upper terraces. Ed took Alice and Edward Graeffe, an Austrian-born family friend, ahead in the small jeep. We came behind in the land rover. When we arrived and our headlights shone on the plaza, there stood the three of them. Alice was in a state of disarray, her skirt high, Edward and Shook with trousers equally out of position. They had stepped from the jeep into a column of marching army ants! Ed had quickly ordered them to step a few feet away, but not before too many hundred of the ravenous varmints had climbed onto all of them. When a migration of army ants is under way, it goes through or over or under whatever it encounters, never around, and devours whatever edible is in its path.

All hands came to the rescue that night and, after some moments of misery, the last of the voracious little creatures was swept off. But through it all not a screech from Alice. Typically, the most she said was "Oh my!" and when it was all over she remarked, "After all, we interfered with their lives and habits." Edward Graeffe, being the stalwart Austrian he is, laughed off the incident. But few are privileged to encounter Alices in their lifetimes.

Water

IN THE very heart of Tikal in ancient times was a huge lake, or reservoir. It dominated the landscape in front of a large palace area. Now it is dry, its manmade dam crumpled into remnants. Heavy forests fill it from the bottom to the tops of its original banks. As our modern camp grew, water became an increasing cause of concern. During the rainy season, from May until October, more than a hundred inches fell on the city. The parched ground took its share, but most of the precious water ran off into jungle oblivion. By mid-season our need became acute.

There seemed nothing to do but drill for subterranean deposits, which we hoped were there. We purchased, at a price which dented our budget for that year, a small gasoline-driven drilling outfit which would give us a large enough hole to accommodate four-inch pipe. If the machine could be sold afterwards in Guatemala, we would not suffer too much.

The machine arrived in Barrios, was brought in sections to Tikal, along with the pipe. Then our troubles began. We had trained our masons, carpenters, mechanics, even truck and bulldozer operators, but drilling machine operators? Not one of our men knew how to, as they say, make hole. It was a debacle from outstart. Drilling tools were damaged, holes drilled crookedly, and the average depth per day just a few feet. But again the Tikal gods were smiling. A year before I had met in Havana one Tex Brewer. Tex was in charge of all Latin American operation of Standard Oil, New Jersey. His company had some leaseholds near Tikal in the rain forests and savannahs of the Peten. He had been to Tikal and liked it. When we had talked in Havana he told me that he would be happy to lend a hand if he or his men could at any time. Off I went to call Tex. "Tex, we are in a bad mess at Tikal. We have a small drilling outfit but we don't know how to work the damned thing and we can't train the men. What can you do?" Came the reassuring answer, "Don't do a thing. I'll send you two experts right away, from Guatemala City."

The two drillers were flown in at once. They had the machine going within hours and had drilled through to sea level in three days. But not a drop of fresh water did they meet on the way. They moved the machine quite a distance—same result, and the third time, the same. We abandoned the idea for the moment.

I went back to the States and shortly Percy Madeira called me from Philadelphia. "John," he said, "we have to find water at Tikal. I know a dowser who has had phenomenal success. He will come down for a thousand dollars and help us. But for God's sake, don't make it a museum affair. How could we explain to a scientific body like our own that we had employed a dowser?" I made some snide remark to the effect that I had to agree with what the Museum was anticipated to say, and that dowsers could find water maybe in a pitcher, but beyond that they were pure fakes in my estimation. However Percy persisted and furthermore thought that we should put up the money personally, he, I and a third member of the Museum. We could not have the Museum know officially. So down came the dowser and waved his stupid wand here and there. Finally he marked the spot and we drilled our fourth and last hole. It was dryer, if possible, than the others. Percy didn't mention the dowser much after that. We were able to sell our machine at a fair price to the Government.

"But damn it all," one of the men said one evening, "the Maya had water. Where did they keep it? It had to be cisterned in some fashion and saved from the rainfall." One morning while walking along the road to the main plaza someone saw what looked like a small ditch, man-made. He followed it through the brush for a distance. Other ditches joined it. On it went slowly down hill. Finally it came to what looked now like a filled marsh. Shook cleaned it and there was a man-dug reservoir! How simple; we promptly dug another beside it and had enough capacity to last us many weeks. We were ready for the rains. The Maya had our solution; we had just failed to recognize it.

The discovery brought other ideas to the fore. My little contribution was to ditch each side of the airstrip, then over three thousand feet long, and catch the water from it into a pond dug at the low end. This we did and had ourselves another useful lake. Trik solved the drinking water problem in true expert fashion. Our saw mill was put to work turning out staves and our little machine shop cut and shaped iron bands. Trik drew a plan for two hundred-barrel tanks and the mill hands soon produced the materials. He erected the two tanks near one of the larger office buildings, whitewashed the roofs and put on gutters. We had ample drinking water for the duration of the job.

As the second season ended and the third advanced, word had got around. Tikal should be seen. We were having two, sometimes three, DC-3 plane loads of visitors per week from Guatemala City. They arrived in the morning with their picnic lunches, spent the day, and flew back in the afternoon. Meantime our own personnel was swelling. We urgently needed permanent quarters and good meals for them. Heretofore the kitchen was a smoky shack, pots dangling over an open fire, and a fat sweaty Indian woman preparing the only dishes she knew, corn, beans and chicken, the latter clucking around her feet until their fate overtook them.

Antonio Ortiz was a young, ambitious Petenero (man of the Peten). His wife was a fair cook. His English was good. We talked it over and Shook offered him the contract for feeding our crew of fifteen or more. We would build the dining room and kitchen and furnish them. At the same time, we faced the mounting problem of the visitors. Shook and Trik worked out a way to combine the two. We built the dining room much larger and also built a small lodge, six rooms and twelve beds. Ortiz would run both. He would feed our crew under a contract at a small rate per diem, charge the tourists a fair price for meals and another nominal rate for those who stayed over night.

Ortiz would also become chief guide for the ruins, a necessity by now, to protect our crew from incessant questioning. In a few months he was building additional rooms on his own. People came and refused to leave. We were running one eight-passenger land rover and a flatbed jeep loaded with visitors to and from the ruins twice daily. Ortiz studied the ruins and kept up with details of the activities. He became an excellent and entertaining guide. For us the problem of housing and feeding our crew was permanently solved. Latest reports are that Ortiz intends to stand for the Guatemala Congress. He will do well.

The temples of Tikal were built of cut limestone, secured by lime mortar. The ancient quarries must be nearby, now smothered by centuries of jungle growth. Bedrock under the ruins is solid limestone. Its first yard or so is hard from exposure, but below that it is damp and much softer. Trik offered a day's pay to the man who found one of the old quarries. A few days later we had one. It was unmistakable when cleared of growth and accumulated compost. Several cut stones were lying free of the mother bed and the wide cuts made by the Indians were everywhere across the quarry face. We built a road to the spot and started production exactly where the Maya had stopped almost a thousand years before.

The neolithic Indian cut his stone from the rock face with a rope impregnated with crushed quartz or obsidian. The rope may have been made of shredded palm fronds or tough vine fiber. Two men dragged the rope back and forth across the soft limestone, making a cut about four inches wide, on three sides. When the cut reached the required depth to produce the stone size desired, they drove wedges into the cut, forcing the block to break away from the face. We provided our cutters with old fashioned two-man cross-cut saws, the same principle but with an advanced iron age tool.

To complete the authenticity of the restoration plan Trik built a lime kiln. He stacked great piles of firewood, and tons of broken limestone, erected a flue and started his fire. One man would stoke the fire, another would pile on the limestone chunks and remove the pure white lime when slaked and accumulated. We had our two original building elements.

But materials without skilled hands were worthless. The Maya art of masonry had disappeared with the coming of Spanish "culture." Masons must be developed from our native workmen. Trik thought it could be done. First he selected a small ruined building, one with evidence of a stairway and the usual terraces, the two basic architectural features of Maya temples.

He cleaned one side, hauled in the stone and lime and opened his school of masonry.

Everyone but the apprentices themselves was amazed at how quickly they graduated into skilled artisans. Of course parts of their handiwork collapsed but this was a trial building. From the failures they learned that slovenly made back walls, out of sight, would not support the finished exterior ones, and that a repeat of that style of construction would send them back, with reduced pay, to the labor force.

School was soon out; those graduated in masonry were ready for practical matters. The Temple of the Giant Jaguar ('Teena's Temple, our men liked to call it) was to be the first large pyramid-temple restored. First it must be grubbed thoroughly and all root and live branches removed from between the standing stones. Afterwards the extent of restoration would be decided as it progressed, a sound plan which was maintained throughout all restorations. It was no simple matter working on that temple, equal in height to a fifteen-story building and having a sixty degree slope to the temple room at the top, vertical and twenty-five feet high, 135 feet in all.

The top restoration required scaffolding. The search for that was long and frustrating, frustrating in that I could get no manufacturer to give it to me and finally had to buy it; bitter blow. The magnificently carved wooden lintel which had topped the wide temple door had been ripped out a hundred years before and shipped to Basle, Switzerland, where it rests in the City Museum, incongruous and conspicuous there where the Maya collection is small and comparatively unimportant. I went to Basle and made a futile attempt to have it returned to Tikal where it belonged. I offered the Museum in exchange valuable pieces from Philadelphia which were more related to their collection, but they would not part with the lintel. Finally it was agreed that they would make a cast of the piece if we would send the required materials. We did and the impression finally came to us. We made a durable plastic reproduction of the carving on the lintel and fastened it in its proper position to the bottom of the beam over the door where it rests today. In all candor it looks like the original and will last forever, proof against weather, termites, even vandalism.

The Tomb in Temple One

THE PATTERN of research into mounded ruins is fairly constant; the structures are explored through their centerlines. Tikal was no exception, but tunneling was the only way to attack a tall steep building. To cut through as if it were a high pyramidal cake would have been sacrilege, authentic restoration afterwards next to impossible. Trik decided to tunnel through Temple One at the plaza floor level. This meant digging by hand a tunnel, at least five feet high by wheelbarrow width and over a hundred feet long. It would go through rubble fill which had reverted after more than a thousand years of pressure to pure hard limestone. But it must be done.

The base survey established the length of the tunnel which should be cut through on the center axis from front to back. Even if a tomb were found in the early digging, the tunnel should continue through. The possibility of other structures must be explored. It portended an arduous job by the diggers and one that would require constant supervision. To speed the job Trik relied on the survey and plotted a course from both sides to meet somewhere underground. (They met with rewarding accuracy.) Only one man could work each face at a time.

Hours and days ran into weeks as the men followed the hard floor level towards the center with no sign of a break or a patch to suggest something below. Trik's examination of the main stairway outside had revealed two floor levels on the way up the temple. He put men on each of those, hoping to find a burial of some sort marking a building addition, not an infrequent ceremonial of the Maya. There was nothing.

The tunnel diggers, chopping away with their picks, followed the line marked for them by Trik on the tunnel roof. Finally they could hear each other echoing through the two converging faces. Then, after more than a month they broke through and met under that enormous structure, each protesting naturally that he had outdug the other. Neither had produced for us a telltale bulge or floor cut.

All this took place in 1959. Meanwhile work on restoration was progressing. Our supply of cut building stone grew and the restored terraces were beginning to extend upward in handsome array. By 1962 the restoration on Temple One was completed to the extent planned but the tunnel below was still gaping its challenge to Trik.

His notes of tunnel progress showed a scattered deposit of flint chips several yards in from the entrance. Flint chips of the Maya have one reliable implication, there had been a ceremonial of some sort in the vicinity. Although it meant more days of tunneling through that impacted limestone, Trik decided to follow the chips. He picked up the trail and headed north, right angle to the tunnel.

As the chase progressed the quantity of chips on the floor increased. Finally after twenty-five feet the men came upon the profile of a stairway of an earlier building, same old Maya pattern of superimposing one upon the other. There in front of them lay the capstone of the tomb which had to be, a slab only three feet long and half as wide. Discovery was at hand, but no one knew how great at the moment.

I was then in Washington. Trik knew that this temple and its mysteries were of particular interest to me. He restrained himself from lifting the stone until he cabled me and of course I was on the first plane. Early in the program at Tikal, *Life* magazine had made a donation to the project for an article which they published in 1958. I had promised, if any unusual news story broke, to give the magazine first chance. This tomb could well be just the story. We notified *Life* and received an answer that Fritz Goro, one of their top photographers, was on his way. *The Philadelphia Bulletin* heard of the find and sent a newsman. Central American newsmen appeared in quantity.

There was barely enough air trickling into that small niche at the end of the tunnel to sustain two working men. When the tomb would be opened and to a yet undetermined depth, it would be suffocating. In the coal mines we had a rule of thumb that three right angles in an unventilated aircourse were equal to a barrier. Here we already had two right angles and the third one would be vertical when we descended into the tomb. We had to act quickly. Also we had to provide adequate lighting which meant running electric wiring into the tomb. We considered and discarded various schemes for air. Trik finally came up with the most direct. He laid out a straight course from the outside's nearest point directly to the tomb entrance and drilled a hole just above floor level and about ten inches in diameter through the terraces and right to the spot. Instead of laying an air vent over the long and angular route of the tunnel, we went less than a fifth of the distance. Our mechanic rigged a small fan to a gasoline engine and air began to draw out. This in turn set up a flow of air from outside through the tunnel. Our jungle air-conditioning was in order. We could even smoke. Next we installed a small gasoline-driven generator which provided current for lighting. Now the stone could be lifted.

Our little party for the ceremony included Helen Webster, now Mrs. Trik, Mrs. Josiah Marvel, ranking member of the Museum's Women's Committee, the *Life* and *Bulletin* representatives, a bacteriologist from Smith, Kline and French—and Trik and me. We rigged a small hoist and after Trik had removed the hundreds of flint chips littering the capstone we were ready to lift it.

Slowly, reluctantly, it came away from its setting of twelve hundred years. Those were anxious moments for everyone, but up it came. When the stone was securely laid aside we, in turns, looked into a black vastness while the light was being readied for lowering. Suddenly the great cavity was illuminated. We saw a spacious room some fifteen feet long by half as wide and, as usual, its floor smothered with earth fallen from top and sides. The vaulted roof sloped inward to peak itself at a width equal to the lifted stone slab. Although nothing showed through the heavy earth fall, we knew we had a rich tomb, and most important, it had not been plundered.

We had rigged a ladder beforehand and Trik entered the tomb first. He was followed by the bacteriologist who, decked in sterilized white coat and gloves took samples here and there hoping to recover bacteria which had been dozing for more than a millennium. (He didn't.)

The workmen rigged buckets to rope for hoisting the mass of fallen debris to where it could be carted out by wheelbarrow. Goro with his constantly flashing cameras, black and white and color, proved an invaluable asset to the record. (His article on the tomb appeared in *Life* April 23, 1963.) Slowly the unbelievable treasure trove came into view. Once the overburden was removed, every movement of our trowels seemed to reveal another astonishing bit of adornment of this obviously ranking personage. Without relating our step by step exposure of the tomb's contents, let me list the personal adornment of the deceased:—

The skeletonized body lay on a stone bench slightly higher than the tomb floor. Above his head, on the bench, rested a large polychrome bowl, smashed by the fall but with all its fragments recoverable. The headdress was extraordinary; a round shell the size of a cereal bowl set on his head like a skull cap. The side of the shell just below the rim was perforated at regular spaces. From each perforation had dangled a two-inch square of cut jade almost a quarter inch thick. The jades, suspended over the forehead, probably hung down to act as a jeweled eyeshade. At each ear was a jade earplug perfectly carved and close to three inches across. Around the neck and across the upper chest a jade necklace glistened. It was composed of long tubular jades one half inch or more thick and graduated in length from three to four inches to make them lie flat on the chest. There were six rows of those tubes to a cluster, and seven clusters. Across the midriff was draped a literal scarf of jade balls graduated from marble to egg size. Each one was drilled, indicating that the balls had been assembled into some sort of fantastic bandeau. Each wrist held a beautifully created bracelet of shaped jades, as did each ankle. In the crotch lay one long jade tube and delicately placed at the end was one round white pearl. Beyond the feet, as at the head, lay another large multi-colored bowl. It is a fair estimate that this regal person had on his body alone twelve pounds of jade.

Now a look at how he was made comfortable for the journey. First he was placed on a heavy mat, long since rotted away but its pattern clearly etched in the stone bench. Over his body lay a rectangular robe of precious jaguar skins, which had disappeared also, but was confirmed by the presence of four sets of claws of the animals in good condition and resting in normal positions. To complete this fantasia of interment, in double rows on each side of the body were large pink oyster shells. In each shell lay a large jade bead. The shells were perforated and may well have been attached to the edges of the jaguar-skin robe, like floats on a fish net, to hold it in place. When this high dignitary was laid to rest and before the fallen earth and his own distintegration wrecked the ensemble, it must have been a sight to rival any burial known to the western world.

The floor beside the bier was strewn with pottery of every size and description, too numerous and too varied in size and decoration to enumerate here. At one end Trik found another first, a cache of large bones—mostly femurs and tibias, expertly incised with scenes and glyphs. There were hunting and fishing scenes and myriad figures which from their costuming and implements held in their hands gave our archaeologists highly desireable data on Maya man and his equipment. The hieroglyphs are under intensive study now by Dr. Linton Satterthwaite of the Museum in hopes of clearing some of the many mysteries of Maya writing.

Steadily and expertly Trik measured and recorded the tomb and its contents. Then came the meticulous cleaning and repairing by the staff at the Tikal museum. The museum is now opened and visitors may see the contents of the tomb arrayed there in spectacular fashion. Although Trik's tomb was the first one of such immensity, there have been many others since of varying size and type. Dr. William Coe and his crew have enriched our knowledge of Tikal culture with unbelievably beautiful finds from widely separated burials. Other thousands will never be found.

On the north side of the Great Plaza, behind the front line of smaller temples, Bill Coe had begun his enormous exploratory cut. The profiles of its carefully dug vertical sides began to disclose walls and stairways centuries older than the Late Classic period Trik was preserving at the surface. Down and down went Bill and his eager crew; still no end to the building sequences and the fantastic Maya pattern of superimposing building upon building.

Bill's pit was almost tennis-court size, but still it was frustrating for him when only a segment of a beautifully ornamented doorway or wall would appear. To expose more would undermine and threaten the fine temples at the surface. But we knew that no matter where we stuck the spade in that complex of buildings the same unhappy situation would be ours.

At last bedrock and the level of ancient man's beginning at Tikal was reached. There Bill found the telltale postholes which had supported the shelters of men who, he could now determine, lived, worshipped and hunted in that dense rain forest six hundred years before Christ. It was a fine day for Bill, a well deserved success for a brilliant young archaeologist.

Shook's problems mounted as the project grew. We had now reached the status of a small industry there in the jungle. Our labor headaches became acute. Men living in thatched villages throughout the forests left their families on Monday and came to work, sleeping under their improvised shelters around the job. One or two Indian women cooks provided beans and tortillas. When the week ended, the worker took his pay, promptly gambled and drank it away and stumbled, broke and helpless, back to his hungry wife and children. Next week the same performance.

Shook was faced with a wives' rebellion, one he could well condone, and he had the answer. He suggested and we agreed that we build a village. The houses would be given to the best men and those with families. The plan was an instant success. The sawmill turned out long planks of exotic jungle woods that would be unavailable at any price elsewhere, if obtainable at all, mahogany, sapote, etc. We built two rows of houses and closed one end of the little court with two more. One of those became a classroom for children of the workers, the first they had ever seen. The other became the clinic where everyday illnesses and small wounds could be treated.

Shook found a young pharmacist in the city who agreed to fly out during the week. He would administer to the sick and, fine human being that he was, he would also teach school. We built outhouses, each with its lime box. Water was piped into communal tanks, even electricity came to those who had never known anything but an oil lamp or possibly a pinetar torch.

The families were reunited, the women and children assured

of food; happiness reigned. A modern village in the Peten forest; unheard of.

As for me, I had been handed another bit of good fortune, this one so small that at first it required my type of imagination to recognize it. We had a school; tiny, I admitted (twenty-five children), but a school. We had a doctor and we had medicine. Schools and doctors and medicines spelled Rockefeller. I took photographs of the school children, scrubbed and in clean bright clothes, standing proudly with their teacher, the doctor.

I admit now that but for Shook, Trik and Rainey, I would have hurled myself again, like Don Quixote, at the Foundation with my new weapon. "Here are my educational and my medical programs." But these men were thinking too. They knew and sympathized with my long frustration. Their plan was simple and had merit. "Guatemala has no trained archaeologists. Some day our men must leave here. We could offer to train Guatemalan students at Tikal, give them supervised field experience and offer suggested reading. We are training masons, carpenters, electricians, even truck and bulldozer operators, why not supervisors?" Magnificent, constructive and imaginative, this suggestion of our afterguard. Now my arsenal was really stocked; back to the assault on Rockefeller Foundation, now in its fourth year.

But my good friend at the head had departed. President Kennedy had tapped him for Secretary of State. I could comment at length on that move but shall not. My respect for and admiration of the man himself and the loss to the Humanities are difficult subtractions for me to negotiate from the uncertain plus factor of his present eminence.

But Dean Rusk had not lost interest in Tikal. He still hoped that I could find a formula that would penetrate the Foundation's heart and coffers. His successor had not yet been named. Gilman Gilpatrick, in his capacity as head of Humanities, handled such requests as mine, and he was quite familiar with my long-standing appeal for funds. He listened attentively to my most recent plan. He was impressed with the sums we had raised without Rockefeller. He would suggest that a committee of two come to Tikal!

Once we get a prospective donor to visit Tikal words are superfluous. The wondrous old city sells itself. The Rockefeller representatives quickly appreciated the education and health advancements already made and realized the need for student training. They returned to New York and recommended participation to the Rockefeller Foundation. After the long discouraging campaign I had my reward, the largest single grant by any donor.

Tikal was solidly on its feet now. Avalon Foundation approved my request for another fifty thousand dollars: Mrs. Scaiffe continued her interest and help. Teena saw her temple to a highly praised completion. My bit part at Tikal was over.

The huge program was to continue another five years under the Museum's directorship. Changes were to occur in our own personnel, but the final result was ordained; a glorious and important city of the ancient Maya had been brought back for the clear conception of modern man. Guatemala had a national monument of which to be eternally proud. Fantastic tombs laden with the Maya arts in pottery, stone, obsidian and jade rewarded the trowels of our archaeologists. A fine museum now stands where monkeys and jaguars leaped through the high trees. The Guatemala Government has now picked up the mantle of supervision and finance, and the work will continue in the capable hands of its own archaeologists and architects. We hope the restored Tikal comes near to what Ted Kidder dreamed of that day years before at Zaculeu, when he challenged me. He saw and approved the early stages but did not live to appraise the final.

Gordion

"A City of the Phrygian Kings"

By 1960 the time had come to examine and weigh the idea of other big, long-running productions, and my participation. Tikal continued to move into immortality. Thousands of visitors came to see and marvel at its former grandeur, now being skillfully unearthed and preserved. Possibly something would come along with a challenge, but with the inducement of a shorter run. I felt a bit like the old character actor, standing in line at the caster's office, asking for a small part perhaps, but with a short run; no more extravaganzas with long stands in one locale. Maybe there was something in a new land with an opportunity for broadened experience.

Froelich Rainey is a relentless agent. "I have an idea for our dig in Gordion, Turkey," he announced one day at the Museum. "If I can persuade Rodney Young, maybe you would go over there and test the idea." (Rodney Young is head of the Mediter-

Gordion

ranean Section at the University of Pennsylvania Museum and is Director of the Museum's Expedition to Gordion.)

Gordion is in central Turkey, west of Ankara. It is named for ancient King Gordius. A Greek myth tells of the Phrygians learning from an oracle that the man who would become the new king was coming their way in an oxcart. He would alleviate their woes and restore their happiness. Gordius was a simple peasant who happened to arrive presently in his cart. He became King.

Overcome with gratitude, the new king offered his wagon to Zeus. He laced the wagon's pole to the yoke with a knot so complex that it could not be loosened by any one of the many who tried. Thus it became the "Gordian knot" and the one who solved it would become master of all Asia.

It withstood all attempts until the arrival of Alexander. That young and restless conqueror had no time for methodical effort. With one slash of his sword he "cut the Gordian knot," an expression preserved and used today, after more than two thousand years, "to devise and use instantly a drastic way out of a difficulty."

The Phrygians came from the Balkans and settled at Gordion circa 1200 B.C. They flourished until the middle of the sixth century B.C., when they were overrun by the Cimmerians, an ancient people from south Russia. It was that affluent period before the Cimmerians that Rodney Young was exploring at Gordion.

Rainey's scheme was simple and direct. Young agreed to test it. The rich tombs of the Phrygian Kings were dug into the earth of the flat Turkish plains. They were heavily timbered on all sides and roof. When the king or man of prominence was ceremoniously buried and the tomb closed, the Phrygians carried in thousands of tons of clay and built a chocolate-drop-shaped pyramid of the sterile fill over it, sometimes to the height of nearly two hundred feet and well over five hundred feet in diameter at the base.

Today those pointed mounds may be seen singly along the

railroad, miles west of Ankara and continuing to where they are massed near Gordion. Rodney Young had dug a number of them. In 1957 the archaeological world was astonished by the discovery of a prodigious and richly furnished tomb which Rodney had tunneled into, instead of attempting to remove a vast amount of hardened clay from the top. But tunneling or cutting from the top by hand was costly and slow. Young knew from experience that the mounds themselves contained nothing of historical value. He agreed that there was no chance that a mechanized approach would destroy treasures or evidence. Rainey's plan was to use a small diesel shovel or bulldozer and cut a slice out of a mound down to a critical level, stopping before there was any chance of a cave-in. From that point the laborers would continue by hand. Why didn't I go to Gordion, try to lease a machine and operator, and test the method on a mound Rodney would select?

Froelich Rainey is happiest when he is moving his pawns a few thousand miles to new ventures. After a short visit to Tunisia, not exactly the direct route to Turkey, Teena and I jumped to Rome, where I left her until I could examine Gordion's accommodations and decide if she should follow. I flew to Istanbul and on the following day to Ankara. From Ankara to Gordion is about four hours by train. I was met there and driven over the steppes to the site where Rodney Young had been digging so successfully for nearly a decade.

Next day it was decided that I would return to Ankara and try to charter a small diesel shovel preferably, if not, a bulldozer. Turkey at that time was in economic turmoil. Its currency had deteriorated on the world market, all imports were prohibited. Even government machinery was breaking down from lack of parts. Taxi cabs and buses starved for such essential replacements as spark plugs and tires. If there was anything in the nature of my needs, we probably could not trust it to run long enough to do our project. But again my gods chose to be kind.

Walking along a back street of Ankara I saw what had to be

an apparition; on a vacant lot stood a new, bright yellow diesel shovel! It had a three-quarter yard bucket poised as if restless to be about its business. It literally had not lifted a pound of earth since arriving from far away midwestern America. Its half-tracks even were unsoiled.

The mechanical creature was unattended. We sought the Museum Curator, staunch friend of Rodney, and with his help we found the owner. Yes, he owned the shovel but he had not hurried to use it because of the impossibility of getting repair parts should he need them. But our offer with its American generosity was above his will to resist. He agreed to load the shovel onto a truck and bring it to the ruins where he would demonstrate it. If it failed to meet our needs, we would pay for his time out and back. He would come in two days.

We returned to Gordion, I elated, the others skeptical about our man's arrival at all. But he did come, bringing barrels of fuel oil on the truck along with his vicious little yellow monster. He cranked it into action, ran it off the truck on an improvised ramp, lowered the shovel into position and attacked the hard packed clay at the base of one of the mounds. The work of the ancients was no match for that modern instrument of destruction. Large chunks broke away and were systematically lifted and tossed aside. All hands were convinced, and we were ready to have it climb the steep side of a selected mound and gnaw its way down from the top.

Early next morning we watched the lumbering machine steadily climb the mound, poise as if to take a breath, then drop its toothy jaw into the clay. Across it went until it had a mouthful, then spat it over the side and turned hungrily for another. Rodney smiled with approval. That first day we moved more than two hundred yards of clay, leaving a neatly carved trench. (That was about what a dozen men could dig and carry away in a week.) Next day the yardage doubled.

The Phrygians had contrived to supply air for their illutrious buried dead by installing a tube of bamboo sections some four or five inches in diameter. It ran from the tomb roof vertically to the mound surface. There the outlet was cleverly concealed to prevent robbers from finding it and following it downward to the tomb. For additional deception they never placed the tomb directly under the mound's proposed center, but in a remote and unlikely sector. With the centuries the bamboo decayed and disintegrated, but the telltale hole in the clay remained.

Thus finding the hole was tantamount to a cross section of the mound and its truant burial. Modern drill holes would then define the tomb size and shape, and from it the alignment of the necessary cut could be established. For us the hole appeared towards the end of the second day of digging. It could now be followed down by machine until Rodney judged the shovel's weight would cause a cave-in, whereupon his men would take over with hand tools.

The prospect of playing a small part in unearthing one of Gordion's tombs was thrilling. Equally exciting to contemplate was the opportunity of watching Rodney handle the final approach and opening.

But that was not to be. My friendly genie who had protected me for so long was to fail me on the plains of Gordion. I had recognized the symptoms a day or two before. That night my lurking ulcer threat erupted into violent bleeding. I was through. Next morning Rodney had me driven to Ankara where I took a plane back to Rome.

I had cabled Teena of my precipitous return, but without explanation. However, long experience with me and my malady warned her. She met me with a car, and after a look knew the answer. Rome is blessed with a magnificent hospital, the Salvador Mundi. Next morning Teena presented me there for tests, X-rays and the routine which had become too regular during the past ten years. The tests disclosed the latest member of my collection, a whopping cavity just ready to perforate. Two weeks minimum in bed was the order by "Dr. Nick", Head Surgeon at Salvador Mundi (his name is so difficult that even the nurses call him Nick). Somehow we struggled through those days, me fretting and my Teena exhausting the kiosks on the Via Veneto for paperbacks. Then home.

There was small recompense from learning that the tomb was comparatively unexciting. Gordion continues, under Rodney's expert supervision, to give up its past.

The sheep roam the steppes during the day, herded by the giant Karabas dogs. At night the dogs sweep them into line and corral them into their respective villages where they are rounded into a tight circle with the dogs posted like alert sentries on the periphery.

The camel trains come snaking into view miles away across the dunes. They pass noiselessly, except for the muffled stamp of their padded feet on the sands. Each camel carries his two hundred pounds saddled across his undulating back. All day from sun-up to sun-down he maintains his steady four miles per hour. The train collects merchandise such as pumice and other Black Sea products and bears them to the Mediterranean. For the return trip it will carry possibly coffee and spices. Little has changed on the steppes of Turkey. It was quite the same three thousand years ago when Gordion was an oasis bejeweled with palaces long since in ruins.

It matters little to these men of the steppes what transpires in Ankara or on the Bosphorus. Their lives, habits and customs are immune to the effects of some futile debate at the U.N. They have survived too many interpretations of empire, mushrooming itself into temporary success only to collapse under the pressure of some neoteric ideology, some design for self-aggrandizement cloaked in a protestation of its being best for the people. Were there mineral treasures in the deep stratigraphy beneath their sandaled feet, no benefits or uplifts would accrue to themselves. Resignation remains the brake upon ambition.

"Take some more tea", the March Hare said to Alice, very earnestly.

"I've had nothing yet" Alice replied in an offended tone, "so I can't take *more*."

"You mean you can't take *less*," said the Hatter: "It's very easy to take more than nothing."

Cycladic Interlude

By 1963 George Huxley had terminated his highly successful visiting Professorship of Greek at Harvard. Both he and the University were reluctant to end the association. But George and his wife Davina are English and were justified in desiring to raise their growing family in the British Isles. George returned, therefore, and accepted the Chair of Greek at Queen's University of Belfast.

Teena and I had come to know and appreciate George's talents during a short acquaintance while we cruised the Aegean Sea together. I visualized him as a permanent member of the Museum's staff in Philadelphia where we sorely needed a Greek archaeologist and scholar.

With Rainey's permission I approached George with a proposal that he secure a permit for a dig in Greece or on one of its insular possessions. The Museum would engage him as chief archaeologist if he could obtain the permit for the summer of

1964. George relished the opportunity for field work to augment his academic activities as do most professors. It was agreed that, if a permit could be had, I would come for the survey and general assistance and that Trik would do his customary research and recording of the tombs.

Huxley was in full harness in no time and soon announced possession of a permit from the British School of Athens to dig a site on the Greek island of Kythera. George had explored the island and was positive that a colonization sequence existed there which could well extend from the Minoan in the second millennium B.C. through to the Roman. It would not be a grandiose operation but would well occupy our limited time during the summer holiday months. It was agreed that we would foregather in Kythera in late June. Kythera is just off the Greek mainland, about a hundred miles south of Piraeus, the port of Athens.

The Minoan civilization on ancient Crete was named for King Minos. It endured through three long periods, Early, Middle and Late, and covered some seventeen centuries from 2800 B.C. to 1100 B.C. King Minos, according to Greek mythology, was the son of Zeus and Europa. He took for himself as wife Pasiphae who bore him four sons.

But Minos fell afoul of Poseidon, the powerful god of the sea and of the fresh waters. Poseidon was famed for his bad temper and evil disposition. He carried the trident which empowered him to cause earthquakes. Poseidon demanded that Minos sacrifice a white bull to him, but Minos refused. Knowing of Minos' love for Pasiphae, the angry Poseidon caused her to become lustfully enraptured with the white bull and by him she bore the Minotaur.

The Minotaur had the head of a bull and the torso of a man. He was caged in the Labyrinth to keep him out of sight from the sorrowing King. Later when Minos overpowered King Aegeus of Athens he exacted yearly tribute from him of seven young men and seven young maidens whom he threw into the Labyrinth for the Minotaur to destroy in his own fashion. But despite all that, Minos was a prosperous and a just man. His name became immortalized by the Minoans.

The Early Minoan culture (2800 to 2100 B.C.) saw the transition from the neolithic to the first use of metals, and introduction of hieroglyphic writing. The Middle period (2100 to 1580 B.C.) brought sophisticated building and writing by pictograph. During this period the Minoans developed pottery and ivory carving, even metal working. Their sea power expanded greatly to extend their influence around the Mediterranean. The palaces of Knossos were built, and some destroyed, toward the end of the era.

In the Late period (1500 to 1100 B.C.) new and more magnificent palaces were erected. Writing was improved and the arts advanced. But the Mycenaean pressure was beginning to be felt. Knossos was again destroyed and after that the Cretan cultural predominance withered there and moved to the mainland.

The Mycenaean civilization, named for the ancient city of Mycenae, flourished about the same time as the Minoan (2800 to 1100 B.C.) and was divided also into Early, Middle and Late. It was identified by historians as the Helladic, from the Greek city of Hellas. The Mycenaeans were great builders also, but they concentrated more on powerful fortifications of huge stones. Such techniques fitted their personal appearance; they were large, ominous-looking warriors with black beards and wearing heavy armor. Homer wrote glowingly of the Mycenaeans.

From those venerable days on, through the first millennium and the Hellenistic glory of Greece into the Roman, Kythera was a small but utilized spot on the charts of the mariners. After the fall of Rome it became just another sedentary island. Its rocky lands were stingy with the farmer, unrewarding to the hungry plucking of the sheep. Its grapes and olives were meager bounty for the work involved. It is a poor island.

Its remittance men depart early in life for Canada or Australia where they work for years, sending their wages back to Kythera. When the bank account smiles and beckons, each returns to marry the girl who has probably already been chosen by him years before and who has waited for him. He is now one of the prosperous men of the small island, sitting with his male friends over coffee, rehashing tales of far off lands.

A close English friend of ours, John Leatham, had lived many years in Greece. He and his wife Maureen had spent three weeks with us on an Aegean cruise. John had been our guide and interpreter. His Greek, both classical and modern, are linguistic perfection. We had listened hungrily to his preparatory talks on board before he led us to the various wonders of the islands. His lighthearted sagas from the country's mythology were delightfully interspersed among the academics of his talks. His own personal adventures added proper seasoning. For instance, he and a friend built from keel up their own sailing vessel and sailed it around the Aegean with light cargo and paying guests who were willing to do their sightseeing the rugged way. At another time he had taken his recording instrument and traveled by foot into the highlands where he lived among the shepherds in order to record their songs.

When Kythera materialized, I persuaded John to come for the first season. He would look after Trik and me while we struggled with the local tongue. He would be invaluable to Huxley by relieving him of logistical worries. Huxley knew John well and was quick to agree to his coming.

Huxley had gone on ahead to Kythera. We were to follow after we had gathered our gear in Athens. A letter from Huxley told us how to get to Kythera, overnight from Piraeus by ship. He had also given us the address of the local ticket office where we would be able to engage staterooms, maybe. Straightaway John proved his worth. He made it all seem so easy. Handsome, six feet, blonde, when he stood before the pretty little dark-haired ticket girls and came forth with their own language spiced with

Cycladic Interlude

his cultured overtones, they wilted into admiring submissiveness. Tickets were in hand in no time with the best staterooms available.

The day before I had persuaded the American Air Force Headquarters in Athens to lend us a variety of supplies and equipment for the life of the expedition. The Major was gratifyingly cooperative. "A warehouse near the offices has held monstrous inventories since the end of the war and you can certainly make use of whatever is there and useful." My list of wants didn't faze him. He came forth with:-

- Two 4-man tents with storm covers
- Four cots
- Four mattresses and sleeping bags
- One unopened case of canteens and ration kits
- One case of K rations and other canned goods
- Four acetylene lamps with fuel
- One theodolite, steel tape and level rod
- One axe
- Small tools, even toilet paper.

The lot would be loaded by the military into a truck and delivered to the pier the next morning, before departure. We were awaiting it when it rolled onto the pier.

Trik and I stood in awe, completely useless, as John took over. He recruited ship's hands and bossed them like a stevedore. In unbelievable time he had the entire load on board and safely stowed. While he was hustling the men through that job he had time to clear us and our own luggage through the red tape of port authority and ticket takers' bureaucracy and into our cabins. Thank the Greek gods for John Leatham!

With a plaintive toot the ancient vessel pulled out into the twilight bound, by wayports, to Kythera, scheduled for next evening. The *S.S. Myrtidiotissa*, her rusty sides glaring shamelessly through the sporadic remains of what had once been white paint, her inadequate lifeboats dangling from blackened lines, this single screw antique was not too reassuring. We could barely make out the name on the pilothouse. "What does the name Myrtidiotissa mean in English?" we asked John.

"The Myrtle Garlanded One," he replied, getting the laugh he deserved.

We landed next evening at the port of Kapsali. Amidst the confusion which attends ship arrivals even in ports accustomed to it, we were shoved and shunted ashore by the returning voyagers. Most had simply been to Athens but for them it was probably their first venture from their native Kythera, nothing short of world adventure. With hands full of native flowers and with tearful papas and mamas expressing relief and joy over a safe return, they struggled ashore with their valises held together with twine and their bulging cotton bags over shoulder.

George Huxley met us with a 1930 vintage Ford. He had commandeered a truck for our expected cargo of equipment and as in Piraeus, John had it off and loaded and secured again promptly, all pieces counted and checked.

It was then after ten. We bumped along a narrow road for half an hour to the inland village of Khora and a small inn. Here we would spend the night. The Greeks have accustomed themselves to late hours and this was not too far into the night for Mrs. Daponte, the owner, to greet us with the charm and good humor of a successful innkeeper. We sat down to a hot dinner on immaculate linen in a small dining room that smacked of good housekeeping. Hot soup, spaghetti, with excellent cheese and mutton, followed by a variety of fruits and tea, put us in humor for bed. Down the narrow hall was a shower room with hot water and inside facilities, both a mild surprise.

Our coming experience across the island at Kastri, our site on the shores of the Aegean, was not to be too uncomfortable if this were an example. But we knew better; deserted ruins overgrown with olive groves are not expected to rank with modern Greek villages like Khora. John and George had found a night

Cycladic Interlude

watchman for the truck and contents. Next morning we were off in the car and truck across the island to our site on the shores of the Aegean.

George had engaged the grove owner and his wife, a happy Greek couple, to feed us and provide space for our equipment. Actually, George had persuaded the couple to give up one of their small rooms, of which they had only three, to him and one of his students as a bedroom. We unloaded the truck under the shade of a willow. It was just after seven a.m. but I was suddenly aware of the temperature. The thermometer was licking the underside of its ninety degree mark and it was just breakfast time!

We sat for a moment under an arbor in front of the little house, where we were to have all meals, while the men struggled with the tent. I looked enviously at the younger men around me (who doesn't?) and thought of my chances for running a survey over the steaming rocks in heat such as this. Tea and cookies were produced and over them George explained the plan of campaign.

From ten-thirty or eleven until four o'clock the temperature would be around 110 degrees, not a compatible working climate for any of us. Therefore we would rise at five-thirty, breakfast at six and work until nine. We would return for a second breakfast, after which we would siesta or loll on the beach where we could languorously roll into the comparatively cool waters of the Aegean, 85 degrees. Then after lunch we would repeat the late morning laziness until four when the slant of the sun would weaken it back to ninety and we could continue our chores until dark. It was a sensible plan and one that even the youth of the party relished.

We reconnoitered the area until lunch time. Trik and I decided on where we would run our baseline for the survey, then George took us up the sloping hillside, where he pointed out the tomb area. One of George's two student helpers from England was a fine Irish lad named Fred Daugherty. Fred was ambitious to become an archaeologist and thought George the man to emulate; certainly not a bad choice. He was to become my bearer, carrying the heavy theodolite whenever it was moved. He scorned the heat and never quite understood the long periods of rest between what he considered light work.

When we returned to the house the tent was in position, thanks to John and crew. It had been up just long enough to be preheated by the noonday sun. Sam Magee's cremation must have taken place in some similar manner. We realized that it would be next to lethal, if not entirely, to attempt sleeping under that scorching canvas. Worse still, there was no shade where the tent could be reset. Small olive trees just will not protect army tents. It was a breathless, relentless oven. But the Greek gods are compassionate!

Trik had spotted a tiny mud hut a hundred yards or so from the owner's. It was the home of a young woman who worked in the grove. It had thick walls, a tile roof, and a modicum of shade from the west. John was put to work. His persuasive smile and words about how the Americans really did demand so very much, but they were willing to pay, soon had the poor girl willing to move out and give the shack to Trik and me. Our cots were carried in and we, of course, had no hesitation in confiscating the woman's one chair. A packing box became the dresser, and the washstand was set up just outside the door on another box. A stretched cord between two olive trees carried towels for drying. We were housekeeping.

The privy had been dug by George's men, a fairly remote one-holer with burlap walls, box for paper, and the inevitable lime sack. The dispossessed woman agreed to come and do our beds and wash our dirty digging clothes. We rigged a shower by perforation of a gasoline drum raised onto a low platform and fresh water poured into the top. It served to desalt us after the sea bath. We were a gay and compatible lot, once we had matters in hand.

Excavations at Kastri were never to be heavy. The earth over-

Cycladic Interlude

burden atop the solid rock was too thin, after many centuries of erosion, to conceal structures of important proportions. But the proof of early occupancy was definitely there. We laid out our baseline along the shore where we could project a long straight line up the beach. We then worked our survey lines inward, placing solid benchmarks at selected locations. From those I could triangulate large areas without having to chain the long hot lines. Slowly we developed the map of the immediate neighborhood where George was to dig for house evidence and Trik to search for burials.

Huxley had found the burial grounds quite by accident. In fact they had been discovered for him by reckless use of a bulldozer cutting across the valley. The ancient settlers had cut their crypts into the soft sandstone and closed the entrances with boulders. The modern road builders had ruthlessly cut away the hillside, exposing the first of the burials. Naturally those had been looted by the road men, but we hoped for others untouched. The desecrated ones stared up into the Aegean sky with huge sightless eyes reddened by the glare of the relentless sun.

But, even empty, the tomb types were new and stimulating to Trik. He set about drawing selected types just to get the feel of them. Later digging rewarded him with several unmolested graves. The burials were not richly furnished compared to those we were accustomed to in other research, but they provided Huxley with ample information for dating the site and determining from where its people came.

George and his associates, Richard Hope-Simpson and Nicholas Coldstream, had selected their area for excavations. It was on a low hillside where George had detected surface sherd material. It sloped downward to a low bluff rising from a dried riverbed which we agreed could well have afforded access from the sea in ancient times. Later George was to confirm our deduction by unearthing large cut stones in the river bed which were most certainly part of a dock. We tied the excavation area into the survey, and Huxley and Hope-Simpson set about dividing the plot into a series of quadrangles to give each man a controlled section for his digging.

Straightaway we learned from Huxley what was, for Trik and me, a departure from the tedious and laborious method of handling potsherds which has prevailed in our hemisphere for so long. At our excavations the diggers collect, wash and bag literally millions of pieces of broken pottery for "future study." There is positive proof that hundreds of those bags have not been opened for many years and it is doubtful if they will ever be opened. This waste of time is the direct result of either uncertainty on the part of the digger or his reluctance to declare himself. In either case he could well be accused of lack of familiarity with his subject. Not so with Huxley.

That young man knew his field and proceeded with confidence. In the evening the sherd baskets, each with its location tag, were brought in and dumped in front of George on a large table. While his men took notes, George went through the lot, basket after basket. He would call out the period, style and date of significant pieces, confidently sweeping away the useless majority. Those kept were tagged and filed. It was a skillful performance and one to impress his students. Certainly it would have been a profitable lesson for some of our oldtimers on how to adroitly save time and reduce storage and transportation problems.

The nearby Aegean was another charitable provision of the gods. Every few hours we splashed into its comparatively cool waters, to reduce body temperatures and deliver back to the salty sea our encrusted perspiration. Using it for our giant bathtub was incidental. John and George swam what seemed forever to us dog paddlers. With a bar of Lava soap in hand, I was content to wallow waist deep and conserve my energy for the shorebound activities.

Somehow we all remained healthy throughout that sweltering summer. My own work was soon finished. The mapping had progressed to where Huxley's trenches and Trik's tombs could be accurately located. Cross sections and elevations were complete, contours were drawn in; now I could conscientiously consider leaving. Leatham felt the call of his neglected farm which he had left behind to generously donate his help to me and the project. We departed shortly, leaving Trik and Huxley and the others to put the dig to bed for the balance of the year. Fall terms would soon demand everyone's return. Kythera's first season was near its end.

Trik rejoined Huxley the next summer and brought his beautiful and talented wife, Helen. Helen is not only an intrepid companion, but is a capable woman around any archaeological project. At Kythera she assisted Trik with his recording of burials, and produced her own expert photographs. Helen's stamina and resourcefulness have stood the test of many remote and wretched circumstances around the world.

The digging was completed in that second summer and, although the finds were not spectacular, they proved beyond doubt that Kythera was one of the waypoints of Minoan and Mycenaean culture on its journey from Crete to the Greek mainland; furthermore, that the little island was occupied from 2000 B.C. through the fifth or sixth century A.D., when the Romans took control, to modern times.

Kythera was not intended to be a major expedition. After two sizzling summers of digging, and two more when Huxley returned to combine a "vacation" with writing his reports, the project ended. For me it had been a new departure in archaeology. The suffocating heat of the day, the muggy restlessness of the nights, and the rather limited diet were not too much to pay for the privilege of exposure to George Huxley's knowledge and his impelling manner of imparting it. One can not become a Greek scholar in two months, but the seed was planted, too late in life to flower properly. After all, a bit player in Greek drama hardly expects the lead in "Agamemnon."

Experience in Etruria

THE MEN and women of the University of Pennsylvania Museum have pioneered numerous departures in technique in archaeology, an impressive number during the postwar years. By pioneering we do not necessarily imply that all the methods themselves are original to our Museum and staff. Some have been ideas of others which we have adapted to the fields where, by testing under working conditions, the instrument or system can be evaluated. With that practical experience, quite often we have been able to correct and improve.

Dr. Froelich Rainey, Director of the Museum, ably assisted by our Museum technical staff, has encouraged and promoted any method or system which has offered the slightest possibility of advancing our science. Other institutions here and abroad have also contributed enormously. As a result, newspapers and magazines here and everywhere have carried so many articles on carbon 14, for example, that that method of dating has become drawing-room conversation. The average reader nowadays speaks knowingly about radiocarbon being absorbed by all growing things, animal or vegetable. Our occasional dinner partner can discuss with us how, after death, organic matter gives off carbon 14 in countable rays, thereby reducing its own content regularly, and that those rays can now be counted to determine age.

Radiocarbon 14 was the spectacular beginning of a series of dating methods. Although it functions only with deceased animal or plant life, it was able to revolutionize heretofore accepted dates and send the historians scurrying for erasers. We simply did not know how wrong we were. We have estimated for years that the last glacial period was some twenty thousand years ago. Now we know it to have been just half that, only ten thousand years since our northern lakes and rivers were gouged out of the rock by the ice packs. Revelations such as these deliver quite a jolt to old theories and methods. Architecture and city life existed in Jericho, where the walls came tumbling down, in the eighth millenium B.C., a date which would have been met with derision before carbon 14—and still is by some biblical hardheads who swear by the Book.

The scope of our dating methods grows surprisingly. Now we are working successfully with systems involving ancient pottery and such neolithic materials as flint and obsidian. It is difficult for you and me to comprehend an apparatus which can measure the incrustation on an arrowhead so accurately that the time of its original flaking can be determined, even back to a half million years ago.

Such modern tongue twisters as thermoluminescence are tossed off today when the physics lab wishes to describe the luminous properties remaining in a potsherd which will give them the time when it was fired. Another, the potassium-argon method is smugly reserved for the times when we please to deal with a million years or more. So we advance.

But before we can employ any of these or other methods,

we must discover our samples and classify them positively with the civilization or culture we are exploring. This ability is basic with the archaeologist. Let us suppose the unlikely event that our worst fears materialized and we were bombed into oblivion. Then, to carry the metaphor a thousand years farther, a new breed of archaeologist comes on the scene. His reference books, of course, have disappeared with the holocaust. In his course of digging he comes upon the home floor of a twentieth century family—shall we say the living room. He finds remains of some contemporary furniture; in one corner huddles a tangled mass of glass and wood and wire which had produced Cronkite, or a futile meeting of the U.N. This our new scientist expected, but what is this in the hall corner? A table or chest of some sort, charred beyond recognition, but from bits he decides it was not the same vintage as the preponderance of the furnishings. He has no way of knowing that that piece was an heirloom handed down for generations, or picked up at an antique sale. But if the laboratories are still in business or new ones have developed, he takes his pieces to the physicist and carbon 14 reveals beyond a doubt that the tree for the old piece was killed and made into lumber three hundred years before the tree that was laminated into the cabinet for the TV.

Similar circumstances occurred among the ancients with one important exception: some of their surviving objets d'art are more likely to be found in their tombs; their homes are gone.

The prevalent system for searching out burials is no different from what it was a hundred years ago; where there was a mound or ruined temple structure there should be one or more tombs, quite often on the centerline of the building. But what about burial grounds?

By 1960 it was proven that the mysterious Etruscans had buried many of their dead in a necropolis in western Italy near the village of Tarquinia, and in another reserved area near Cerveteri known as Monte Abbatone. The cemeteries had been discovered long ago and a number of tombs had been systematically looted. Fortunately the Italian Government had condemned the area and stopped the promiscuous robbing.

At that time a man came on the scene of Italian archaeology who was to make a lasting imprint. His name was Carlo Maurilio Lerici. Dr. Lerici had developed a highly profitable business of fabricating metals in Milan after the war. His hobby was archaeology and the application to it of scientific methods. He created the Lerici Foundation within the Milan Polytechnic School.

Dr. Lerici was familiar with the proton magnetometer, devised by scientists of Oxford University for detecting buried structures or other anomalies. The principle of the Oxford discovery was that the earth's magnetic intensity was steady, varying only in different localities. But the natural intensity in any one locality was an invariable. The magnetometer performed by detecting unnatural variations beneath the soil which could be suspected of being man-made. To go into the details of the invention here would make for laborious reading. It is how Dr. Lerici and his trained crew employed the magnetometer that added new luster to the detection device and its collateral possibilities.

We were invited to Tarquinia to witness these exciting new appliances in operation. Dr. Lerici drove us from Rome to the necropolis near Tarquinia, some seventy miles north of Rome. The other burial ground at Cerveteri was close at hand. The tomb areas had been surveyed, then tested by magnetometer; they were literally honeycombed with vaults cut into the soft stone. Examination of the tombs previously opened foretold the expected shapes and sizes of the undisturbed ones. They were either rectangular or square with an occasional long narrow room adjoining. The entrance was through a doorway which sat at the bottom of a crude stairway. After use the stairway had been filled with loose rock, effectively closing the tomb. It was those stone-filled stairways which were easily detected by the magnetometer, because of their relatively high resistivity compared with the indigenous ground.

More than 650 tombs had been located and mapped at Cerveteri and an unbelievable 4000 at Tarquinia. But how to inspect, economically, such a vast number when the odds were that a huge percentage would be barren, looted in past centuries? It was unthinkable to excavate each one in search of those undisturbed. Then was when Lerici's genius came into play and this was what we had come to Tarquinia to see in operation. It was all so simple, once explained and demonstrated.

First a tomb is selected, the magnetometer having told us where it lies and its depth below the surface, varying from ten to twenty feet. A specially constructed auger powered by a small portable motor drills a hole about five inches in diameter straight down until it breaks through the tomb ceiling. The auger is withdrawn, leaving a smooth hole in the overburden.

Next on the scene is the first of the Lerici surprises, an inverted periscope. It is just that, an aluminum tube fitted with prisms and an eyepiece. On the lower end, which is inserted into the tomb, is fitted a strong light which can be turned on and off from the surface. Shielded in the periscope, it shines in only one direction, to increase its intensity. The observer simply puts his eye to the periscope eyepiece, turns on the light and slowly starts rotating the whole affair by walking in a tight circle around the hole. A 360-degree panorama of the tomb unfolds. The crew with the auger has, in ten minutes, moved no more than a bushel of earth to disclose the whole periphery below, not a bad compromise with the alternative of moving tons of rock and earth, and consuming days of labor.

Now the real value of the Lerici system is demonstrated. The tomb is empty, vandalized in ages past, not worth opening. In a quarter hour the exploration of that tomb is completed and we look into another, already located and ready for testing. But this time, "Have a look!" invites the periscope operator. Revolving the periscope and walking in a tight circle as we had been taught, we look with wonder. There in the scope each of us in turn gazes at beautifully painted walls with the familiar Etruscan figures in black and red. Pots of various sizes lie on the tomb floor. We have a "find."

Nothing accentuates the value of this device of Lerici's more than the data on the number of Etruscan tombs involved. More than four thousand in the two cemeteries were examined by the periscope system and only sixteen were worth opening and preserving. The usual methods, frustrating and exhausting, would have required huge manpower and years of excavation.

But now that the tomb has been inspected, it must be recorded to show the authorities. That necessity introduces the next intelligent step in the process. The periscope is hauled out and its lower end is fitted with an everyday Minox camera inserted vertically and complete with flash and color film. Down it goes into the tomb. The entire interior is quickly photographed by turning a few degrees after each flash. The film is developed and printed and behold, a strip photograph of the hidden chamber beneath.

Dr. Lerici had no intention of involving himself or his foundation in a program of opening the good tombs. That feature he had already programmed with the Italian Department of Antiquities. He presented his photographs to the Department. The Government crews were brought in and the pile of stone carefully removed from the stairway, leaving the roof intact. Then one could walk into and confirm all that had been seen through that tiny orifice.

First step, as in all good archaeological procedure, was to draw and photograph the contents in situ. Then they were removed and carefully cleaned and deposited in the museum chosen by the government for that particular lot. When the artifacts were safely out and the dust of ages cleared away, the wall paintings were sprayed with a preservative. Next a strong wooden door was fixed at the entrance, a padlock installed, and the key handed to the cemetery guide. From then on the tomb was the property of the Department and became an added attraction for visitors and students. The Lerici system had scored another victory in modern archaeology.

We were intrigued with this new adaptation of the magnetometer. But for our purposes and the far distances where we operated, the detecting device was just too cumbersome and unwieldy. Surely we could reduce the weight and make it adaptable to some of our remote operations. We could not transport a station wagon then needed to carry the apparatus. Rainey was impatient. Back home he induced Texas Instrument Company to tackle the problem. Within a year that company had reduced weight and size, substituted transistors for 12-volt batteries, and we were able to obtain even better results with a packaged instrument which Elizabeth Ralph, our expert in geophysical exploration and Associate Director of Applied Science, could carry on her back like a knapsack. Now we were ready for any long range operation. The revelation in Etruria was a memorable one. The archaeological world owes much to Lerici.

Epilogue

TIME, IN ITS quiet but authoritative manner, has announced the hour for me to consider contentment with smaller parts and briefer stands, such as my few days in Etruria. In anticipation of that inevitable admonishment, I have been rehearsing for it.

There was Sybaris down in Italy's boot, where I lent a light hand to the Museum's search for that vanished city of the idle-rich Greeks. It was pure satisfaction watching our improved magnetometer chart a half mile of buried wall with phenomenal accuracy, later verified by digging. If the city's slightest remains exists, one of these new instruments of detection will eventually find it.

But the Croton warriors in 508 B.C., after razing Sybaris, diverted the Crati River over its remaining stubs of walls. For twenty-five hundred years the river has been dropping its silt, not only on the dead Sybaris but over the broad valley where it stood. So far the central area has eluded the searchers, but perseverance will prevail.

Then there was a wet dreary involvement in Northern Ireland where Bernard Wailes and I carried the flag of the Museum. Wailes is Assistant Curator of our Mediterranean Section, but he is well equipped to understand what we expected to find in that outpost of the bronze age. We collaborated with Queen's University of Belfast in an agenda enveloping excavations at Navan Fort in Northern Ireland. Wailes brought undergraduates and postgraduates, boys and girls from America, and all proved their mettle. The summer rains, the ones which make Ireland verdant, flooded our digging quadrangles so unremittingly that those game youngsters worked the muddy bottoms in their bare feet to save their shoes.

Another memorable adventure took us to the shores of Lake Superior where we joined Dr. Albert Spaulding of the University of Michigan in a search for evidence of Pleistocene man. We chartered a small cruiser wherein Teena and I slept sixty-three consecutive nights together in a forty-inch bunk. You get to know each other fairly well under those circumstances, and we would do it again anytime.

Thus the small parts with short runs, lacking challenge years ago, are now promoted to a position of flavorsome tranquilizers as age encroaches. My seventh decade is making rusty, squeaky noises, reminding me that time nears for felt slippers and long boring monologues for my tolerant friends. Such a dictum is unpopular now or any time. We devotees of this dramatic game, archaeology, hang up our tools reluctantly. Like old firehorses, our pulses leap when the bell rings.

In this jeopardous age when the morning news is obsolete by noon, and when international friends of one moment are reduced to the status of uncertain allies the next, I wonder how even veteran writers are able to elect a stopping point. Perhaps a student of the past should confine his text to the past and not

Epilogue

attempt to project his opinions into modern political aberrations.

But when the success of our work is so dependent upon mutual trust and common purpose, it is not easy to remain silent when those values are endangered by statesmen's misbehavior. I am left gasping over the untimely happenings since writing the chapter on our work in Egypt. I spoke then of political matters and how, in my opinion, our United States had bungled our opportunity to gain friendship and respect from the Arabs. That accusation was put into text long before the rout of all reason which occurred in the Middle East in summer 1967. These sad events in no manner influence me to retract a word of what I first said. On the contrary, they spur and provoke me to enlarge upon my premise.

People of science abhor the intrusion of politics into their work, be it local interference or international. Internationally there should be no borders to inhibit the exchange of useful knowledge. The fruits of helpful research are for all mankind. Unfortunately these dedicated groups exert meager world influence. The prepossession of their members leaves little time for attempting it, even should they so wish.

Russia and the United States have come to exchange weather information including reports from sputniks and satellites. Any country on earth with the proper equipment can pick up from the ether what other countries deduce and broadcast concerning storms, tidal waves, iceberg perils. Then why this medieval lack of rapport among the world's statesmen? What a pity that this one vital science, that of foreign relations, weak and ineffectual as it has been proven, should constrict the others.

At the moment our Museum's crews have been withdrawn from all Arab countries. Their local counterparts in each country are as sorrowful as are we. I have been negotiating for the past year with the Department of Antiquities in Libya on a program for the partial restoration of the fabulous Roman city, Leptis Magna, which rests on Libya's shore. I have made two visits to Libya for consultation with the Government in Tripoli on this important work. It is discouraging to think that all this effort has gone for nothing because of induced hatreds at some level so aloof from ours that it cannot even be reasoned with.

Latin America has often suffered from the same mishandling, the same lackluster approach. We systematically, though unwittingly, seem to build hatreds while trying desperately but unskillfully to create friendships. Good hard trading with sagacity is appreciated in those lands. Buying our way only belittles us. If we lose the Latin republics, it will be the result of promiscuous giving instead of selling. They want to like us, more important, respect us. Frantically tossing money at them causes them to despise us. While dealing from strength, how can we be so weak?

Other sciences of the humanities, medicine for example, would indeed be in a sad state if their accomplishments were jealously guarded behind boundary lines. By God's grace they are not. What is the point of all this? How dare nations dignify their aboriginal behavior by calling it statesmanship?

"Wisdom is the principal thing; THEREFORE get
wisdom: and with all thy getting get understanding."

CC   Dimick, J.
165   Episodes in archaeology
.D5
copy 1